untitled f*ck m*ss s**gon play

kimber lee

Produced by Royal Exchange Theatre,
Factory International
for Manchester International Festival,
Young Vic and Headlong

Royal Exchange Theatre, Factory International for
Manchester International Festival: 24 June–22 July 2023

Young Vic Theatre, London:
18 September–4 November 2023

The first performance of *untitled f*ck m*ss s**gon play* was at the
Royal Exchange Theatre, Manchester, on 24 June 2023.

untitled f*ck m*ss s**gon play

by kimber lee

Afi/Goro	Jeff D'Sangalang
Rosie/Cio Cio	Lourdes Faberes
Evelyn/Richards	Jennifer Kirby
Kim	Mei Mac
Narrator/Brenda	Rochelle Rose
Clark	Tom Weston-Jones

DIRECTOR	Roy Alexander Weise
DESIGNER	Khadija Raza
COSTUME DESIGNER	Loren Elstein
LIGHTING DESIGNER	Joshua Pharo
COMPOSER	Ruth Chan
SOUND DESIGNER	Giles Thomas
MUSICAL DIRECTOR	Tayo Akinbode
MOVEMENT DIRECTOR	Shelley Maxwell
FIGHT AND INTIMACY DIRECTOR	Haruka Kuroda
VOICE AND DIALECT COACH	Caitlin Stegemoller
JERWOOD ASSISTANT DIRECTOR	Caroline Yu
JERWOOD TRAINEE ASSISTANT DIRECTOR	Yanni Ng
CASTING DIRECTOR	Helena Palmer CDG
FACTORY FELLOW	mandla rae
DRAMATURG	Suzanne Bell
BRUNTWOOD COORDINATOR	Chloe Smith
PRODUCTION MANAGER	Helen Mugridge
COMPANY STAGE MANAGER	Mason Walter Cooper
DEPUTY STAGE MANAGER	Pip Hussey
ASSISTANT STAGE MANAGER	Milly Stoddart

*untitled f*ck m*ss s**gon play* was first written and developed with the support of the Lark Play Development Center in NYC in 2017 and in 2018 the Ground Floor at Berkeley Repertory Theatre. The play was also developed during a residency at the Eugene O'Neill Theater Center's National Playwrights Conference in 2019 (Wendy C. Goldberg, Artistic Director; Preston Whiteway, Executive Director). The play also received a workshop at the 2019 Ojai Playwrights Conference.

Jeff D'Sangalang (Afi/Goro)

Jeff D'Sangalang's stage credits include: *The Ocean at the End of the Lane* (West End/National Theatre); *That Pesky Rat* (Chichester Festival Theatre); *Shut Up I'm Dreaming* (National Theatre UK tour/ The Pappyshow); *Boys* (The Pappy Show).

Lourdes Faberes (Rosie/Cio Cio)

Actress and filmmaker Lourdes Faberes film credits include: Neil Gaiman's *Anansi Boys* (Amazon); *Boiling Point* (Netflix); *Operation Fortune* (Miramax/STX Global); *No Time to Die* (Eon Productions); *Someone You Love* (Zentropa Productions Intl); *Room 204* (Alphaville Pictures); *Spread* (Katalyst Films); *State of Play* (Universal Pictures). Television credits include: *The Power* (Amazon); *The Sandman* (Netflix); *Grenslanders: Floodland* (Eyework Netherlands/Belgium/C4); *Good Omens* (Amazon/BBC 2); *Holby City* (BBC). Her theatre credits include: *Rescuing One's Sister in the Wind and the Dust* (Almeida Theatre); *Richard II* (Shakespeare's Globe); *The Tide Whisperer* (National Theatre of Wales); *Tamburlaine* (Arcola Theatre); *Cruel and Tender* (Young Vic).

Jennifer Kirby (Evelyn/Richards)

Jennifer Kirby is best known for her role as Valerie Dyer in *Call the Midwife* (Neal Street Productions). Other TV credits include: *Endeavour* (Mammoth Screen); *Vampire Academy* (My So-Called Company) and *Holby City* (BBC). Her stage credits include: *Henry V and Henry IV* (RSC); *Teddy* (Snapdragon Productions); *The Massive Tragedy of Madame Bovary* (Jermyn Street Theatre) and *Pride and Prejudice* (Regent's Park Open Air Theatre).

Mei Mac (Kim)

Olivier Award-nominee Mei Mac is best known for playing Mei Kusakabe in the world premiere of *My Neighbour Totoro* at the Barbican theatre. Other stage credits include: *Dear Elizabeth* (Gate Theatre); *Five Plays – Tongues* (Young Vic); *The Lion, the Witch and the Wardrobe* (Bridge Theatre); *A Midsummer Night's Dream* (Regent's Park Open Air Theatre); *Under the Umbrella* (Belgrade/Tamasha/Yellow Earth Theatre); *The Hundred and One Dalmatians* (Birmingham Rep). Television credits include: *East Mode* (Comedy Central) and *Call the Midwife* (Neal Street Productions).

Rochelle Rose (Narrator/Brenda)

Rochelle Rose's stage credits include: *Rockets and Blue Lights* (National Theatre/Royal Exchange Theatre); *salt.* (Royal Court/Public Theater, NYC); *The Ridiculous Darkness* (Gate Theatre); *The Mountaintop* (UK Tour); *Cinderella and Aladdin* (Oxford Playhouse); *The Winter's Tale* (Orange Tree Theatre) and *One Monkey Don't Stop No Show* (Kiln Theatre/Eclipse Theatre). Her screen credits include: *Boxing Day* (Film 4); *ear for eye* (BBC Films); *Death in Paradise, Lawful Killing* (BBC One) and *Hood Documentary* (BBC Three).

Tom Weston-Jones (Clark)

Tom Weston-Jones' screen credits include: *Warrior* (HBO); *Sanditon* (PBS/ITV); *Shadow and Bone* (Netflix); *The Terror* (AMC); *Troy* (BBC/Netflix); *Dickensian* (BBC); *Not Safe for Work* (Channel 4); *Copper Season 1 and 2* (BBC America); *World Without End* (Channel 4). Theatre credits include: *Labyrinth, Enlightenment* (Hampstead Theatre) and *The Merchant of Venice* (Almeida Theatre).

Kimber Lee (Writer)

Kimber Lee's plays include *the water palace* (2021 Susan Smith Blackburn Special Commendation); *to the yellow house* (La Jolla Playhouse); *untitled f*ck m*ss s**gon play* (2019 Bruntwood Prize International Award); *saturday* (2022 Colorado New Play Summit, 2022 Susan Smith Blackburn Finalist); *antarctica* (Radio Play for Two River Theatre); *tokyo fish story* (South Coast Rep, TheatreWorks/SV, Old Globe); *brownsville song* (*b-side for tray*) (Humana Festival, LCT3, Long Wharf Theatre, Philadelphia Theatre Company, Seattle Rep, Moxie Theatre, Shotgun Players); and *different words for the same thing* directed by Neel Keller (Center Theatre Group). She has also developed work with Lark Play Development Center, Ground Floor/Berkeley Rep, Page 73, CTG, Denver Center, O'Neill NPC, Hedgebrook, Ojai Playwrights Conference, Seven Devils, Bay Area Playwrights Festival, Great Plains Theatre Conference, ACT Theatre/Seattle, Premiere Stages, and Magic Theatre. Lark Playwrights Workshop Fellow, Dramatists Guild Fellow, member of Ma-Yi Writers Lab, and recipient of the Ruby Prize, PoNY Fellowship, Hartford Stage New Voices Fellowship, 2020-2021 Hodder Fellowship, 2020 Helen Merrill Award, 2020 Susan Smith Blackburn Prize Finalist, 2020-2021 Hodder Fellow, inaugural winner Bruntwood Prize International Award 2019, 2021 Edgerton New Play Award, 2023 Hermitage Artist Retreat Fellow, and 2021 Herb Alpert Award in the Arts. MFA: UT Austin.

Roy Alexander Weise (Director)

Roy Alexander Weise is currently the Joint Artistic Director of the Royal Exchange Theatre. He was the 19th annual winner of the James Menzies-Kitchin Award and directed his critically acclaimed, sell-out production of *The Mountaintop* by Katori Hall at the Young Vic. Roy was nominated at the 2018 Evening Standard Awards for the 'Emerging Talent' Award for his production of *Nine Night* at the National Theatre and in the West End. As Joint Artistic Director at the Exchange he has directed *Cat on a Hot Tin Roof,* and *The Mountaintop.* Other production credits include: *Much Ado About Nothing* (RSC); *Master Harold and the Boys* (National Theatre); *The Trick* (Bush Theatre and UK Tour); *Nine Night* (National Theatre & West End); *Dead Don't Floss* (National Theatre); *The Dark* (Fuel Theatre & UK Tour); *Br'er Cotton* (Theatre 503); *The Ugly One* (Park Theatre); *Primetime* (Royal Court) and *Stone Face* (Finborough Theatre).

Khadija Raza (Designer)

Khadija Raza won The Stage Debut award for Best Designer in 2018 and the Linbury Prize for *Dido* in 2017. Other designer credits include: *Every Leaf a Hallelujah* (Regent's Park Open Air Theatre); *The Flood* (Queen's Theatre); *Talking About a Revolution* (The Barn); *Antigone* (Regent's Park Open Air Theatre); *Julius Caesar* (Shakespeare's Globe & on tour); *Sundown Kiki, Love Reign* (Young Vic); *10 Nights* (Graeae & Tamasha Theatre in association with the Bush Theatre); *Bach & Sons* (Bridge Theatre); *Skin Hunger* (Dante or Die Theatre Company); *Augmented* (Told by an Idiot & Royal Exchange Theatre); *Funeral Flowers* (The Roundhouse & tour); *The Bee in Me* (Unicorn Theatre); *White Pariahs* (R&D at The Albany Theatre).

Loren Elstein (Costume Designer)

Loren Elstein designs internationally for theatre, opera, film and dance. Recent works include: *Once Upon a One More Time* (Broadway); *Migrations* (Dir. Sir David Pountney); *The Magic Flute* (WNO); *Hamlet* and *The Cherry Orchard* with Ian McKellen. Other design credits include: *Primetime* (Royal Court Theatre); *Wonderous Strange* (RSC); *The Man Who Almost Killed Himself* (BBC iPlayer). Costume design credits include: *Rosencrantz and Guildenstern are Dead* (Old Vic, NT Online); *RENT* (20th Anniversary Tour, Michael Grandage Company); *The Lie* (Menier Chocolate Factory) and *Terror* (Lyric Hammersmith).

More info at lorenelstein.uk

Joshua Pharo (Lighting Designer)

Joshua Pharo won the Creative Innovation in Lighting Design in 2018 for his work on *The Claim*. Theatre credits include: *Let the Right One In* (Royal Exchange Theatre); *I Am Kevin* (Wildworks); *Corrina, Corrina* (Headlong); *Kerbs* (Graeae & Belgrade Theatre for Coventry City of Culture 2022); *Jekyll & Hyde, The Odyssey: Episode 5* (National Theatre); *Love and Other Acts of Violence* (Donmar Warehouse); *Extinct* (Theatre Royal Stratford East); *The Litten Trees* (Fuel Theatre); *random/ generations, Crave* (Chichester Festival Theatre); *The Rape of Lucretia* (Royal Conservatoire of Scotland); *Cinderella* (Lyric Hammersmith); *Vassa* (Almeida); *The Colour Purple* (Leicester Curve & Birmingham Hippodrome); *The Rolling Stone* (Orange Tree Theatre); *The Merchant Of Venice, Wuthering Heights, Consensual* (West End); *The Crocodile* (Manchester International Festival). TV & Film credits: *Where I Go (When I Can't Be Where I Am)* (China Plate Theatre).

Ruth Chan (Composer)

Ruth Chan is a renowned composer for film, theatre, opera and concert music. Theatre and live work credits include: *Further than the Furthest Thing* (Young Vic); *The Doncastrian Chalk Circle* (National Theatre); *The Hatchling* (The Platinum Jubilee Pageant); *Beauty and the Seven Beasts* (The Opera Story, Brixton Jamm); *Mokita* (Hong Kong Arts Festival); *Strange Tales* (Traverse Theatre/Grid Iron Theatre); *Hedda Tesman* (Chichester Festival Theatre); *The Taming of the Shrew* (RSC); *The Triumph of Time* (Thailand International Composition Festival, Pianoforte Studio Chicago); *Between Constellations* (Pittsburgh Opera Festival & Grimeborn Festival); *Mountains: The Dreams of Lily Kwok* (Royal Exchange Manchester) and *Snow in Midsummer* (RSC – nominated for The Stage Debut Award for Best Music, 2017). Ruth's soundtrack for *Around China With A Movie Camera* (British Film Institute) has been performed at Flatpack Film Festival and Royal Festival Hall. She has also composed for numerous television documentaries. Ruth's re-orchestration of Puccini's *Madam Butterfly* for Opera Up Close toured nationally in 2020.

Giles Thomas (Sound Designer)

Giles Thomas was nominated for Best Sound Designer for the Offie Awards in 2015 for his work on *Pomona*. Composer & Sound Design credits include: *The Contingency Plan* (Sheffield Theatres); *The Almighty Sometimes, The Glass Menagerie* (Royal Exchange); *An Octoroon* (Abbey Theatre, Dublin); *Fair Play* (Bush Theatre); *Cat on a Hot Tin Roof*

(Leicester Curve, ETT & Liverpool Everyman & Playhouse, UK tour); *Romeo & Juliet* (Regent's Park Open Air Theatre); *The Comeback* (West End); *The Dumb Waiter* (Hampstead Theatre); *Marvin's Binoculars, The Twits* (Unicorn Theatre); *Faustus: That Damned Woman* (Headlong, Lyric Hammersmith & Birmingham Rep); *Master Harold and the Boys* (National Theatre); *Equus* (Stratford East, ETT UK Tour, West End); *Plenty, Cock, The Vortex* (Chichester). Sound Design credits include: *Private Lives* (Donmar Warehouse); *The Weatherman, The Ugly One, A Dark Night in Dalston* (Park Theatre); *Tao Of Glass* (Manchester International Festival); *Hijabi Monologues* (Bush Theatre); *Disco Pigs* (Trafalgar Studios & Irish Rep Theatre NY).

Tayo Akinbode (Musical Director)

Tayo Akinbode is a composer and musical director for theatre, film, TV, radio, circus and community projects for companies including: The National Theatre, The Generating Company, OCT East Shenzen, Almeida Theatre, Littlebigman Films, the Royal Exchange Theatre, Miami Gablestage, New York Public Theater, M6, Storyhouse Chester, Specsavers, and Spirit of the Union UAE fortieth Birthday celebrations in Abu Dhabi. Theatre credits include: *The Baccae, King Lear, Cat on a Hot Tin Roof* (Royal Exchange Theatre); *A Midsummer Night's Dream* (Manchester Youth Theatre); *Grandad Anansi* (Z-Arts); *Robin Hood* (Theatr Clwyd); *The Island* (Elysium Theatre Company); *The Whip* (RSC); *Backyard, Rain Rain* (Bamboozle); *Ruff Tuff Cream Puff Estate Agency* (Cardboard Citizens); *Jungle Book* (Oldham Coliseum); *My Voice Was Heard* (Red Ladder Theatre); *Jack Frost* (TuttiFrutti); *Spike* (The Watermill Theatre/ tour). Television credits include: *The World According To Grandpa* (Channel 5 Milkshake).

Shelley Maxwell (Movement Director)

Shelley Maxwell won the award for Best Choreographer at the inaugural Black British Theatre Awards in 2019 for her work on *Equus*. Theatre credits include: *August in England* (Bush Theatre); *The Secret Life of Bees* (Almeida Theatre); *Best of Enemies* (Noël Coward Theatre); *Tartuffe* (Birmingham Repertory Theatre); *The Time Traveller's Wife: The Musical* (Storyhouse); *Get Up, Stand Up! The Bob Marley Story* (Lyric Theatre); *Best of Enemies* (Young Vic); *J'Ouvert* (Harold Pinter Theatre); *After Life, Master Harold and the Boys, Hansard, Antony and Cleopatra, Twelfth Night* (National Theatre); *Nine Night* (National Theatre & Trafalgar Studios); *Equus* (Theatre Royal Stratford East & Trafalgar Studios); *Tartuffe* (RSC); *Macbeth* (Shakespeare's Globe); *Faustus:*

That Damned Woman (Headlong at Lyric & Birmingham Repertory Theatre); *Cinderella* (Lyric); *Grey* (Oval House); *King Hedley II* (Theatre Royal Stratford East); *J'Ouvert* (Theatre503); *Cougar, Dealing with Clair* (Orange Tree); *Winter, Why It's Kicking Off Everywhere* (Young Vic); *Cuttin'It* (Young Vic & Royal Court); *A Streetcar Named Desire* (Nuffield, Clwyd Theatre Cymru & ETT); *Rules for Living* (Royal & Derngate, the Rose Kingston & English Touring Theatre); *Apologia* (English Theatre Frankfurt). Television/Film credits include: *Anansi Boys* (Upcoming on Amazon); *ear for eye* (BBC/Fruit Tree Media); *Romeo and Juliet* (Sky Arts/PBS/National Theatre).

Haruka Kuroda (Fight and Intimacy Director)

Haruka Kuroda is a British Academy of Dramatic Combat-certified instructor and has fight directed and taught in various theatres, drama schools and workshops in the UK and Europe. In 2020, Haruka completed the Intimacy Coordination Mentoring Scheme for under-represented groups organised by renowned IC Yarit Dor. Fight/intimacy directing credits include: *Miss Saigon* (Sheffield Crucible); *Titus Andronicus* (The Globe); *Starcrossed* (Wilton's Music Hall); *The Woods* (Southwark Playhouse); *All My Sons* (Queens Theatre Hornchurch). Fight directing credits include: *Comedy of Errors* (Mercury Theatre); *Love Letters The Musical, Neville's Island* (Queens Theatre Hornchurch); *The Last Temptation of Boris Johnson* (Park Theatre); *Macbeth, Romeo and Juliet* (Guildford Shakespeare Company); *Pink Sari Revolution* (Curve Theatre); *Kanye the First* (High Tide Festival); *Beyond the Fence A New Musical* (Arts Theatre West End); *Harajuku Girls* (Finborough Theatre); *Yeh Shen, Last Days of the Limehouse* (Yellow Earth Theatre); *Incognito* (Gate Theatre); *Running the Silk Road* (Barbican/Yellow Earth Theatre); *The Ladies Cage* (Finborough theatre); King Arthur (Orange Tree). Intimacy Coordinating (TV & Film) credits include: *Rivals* (Amazon Prime); *Such Brave Girls, Life After Life, Superhoe, Sherwood, Strike: Troubled Blood, Silent Witness* (BBC); *Culprits* (Disney +); *Real Friends* (Sky); *History of a Pleasure Seeker* (Hulu).

Caitlin Stegemoller (Voice and Dialect Coach)

Caitlin Stegemoller is a voice and dialect coach originally from Chicago. She coaches across film, television and theatre and is a senior voice tutor at ArtsEd in London. Most recently: The *Band's Visit* at the Donmar Warehouse and a project for Apple TV. Caitlin holds an MFA in Voice Studies from the Royal Central School of Speech and

Drama and a BFA in Musical Theatre from The University of Arizona. Other credits include: *Ride* (Charing Cross Theatre); *The Jumper Factory* (The Young Vic); *Tick, Tick... Boom!* (The Bridge House Theatre); *The Winter's Tale* (The Maltings Theatre); *Belong* (Clean Break). Caitlin has also coached actors for *Operation Mincemeat* (Southwark Playhouse) and *People Who Knew Me* (radio drama on BBC Sounds).

Caroline Yu (Jerwood Assistant Director)

Caroline Yu trained as a director at LAMDA. Prior to this, she directed extensively at the ADC Theatre, where she was the Director's Rep of the Cambridge University Amateur Dramatic Club. Assistant Director credits include: NDT Untapped and Fringe First Award Winner *This Is Not A Show About Hong Kong* (New Diorama Theatre/Edinburgh Fringe Festival); *Lemons, Lemons, Lemons, Lemons, Lemons* (Harold Pinter Theatre); *Cinderella* (Theatre Royal Stratford East); *4000 Miles* (Chichester Festival Theatre). Directing credits include: Origins Award-winner *Walking Cats* (VAULT Festival); *Yen* (LAMDA); *Unexpected Item in the Bagging Area* (Underbelly, Edinburgh Fringe); *Footlights Pantomime: The Gingerbread Man* (ADC Theatre); *Essentially Black* (Camden Fringe); *Baby, What Blessings* (The Park Theatre).

Yanni Ng (Jerwood Trainee Assistant Director)

Yanni Ng has recently completed her final year studying Drama at the University of Manchester, she's been involved in several productions for their Drama Society. Currently, Yanni is working on a new play, *Behind the Curtained Door*, which is going on a university tour in June 2023. *untitled f*ck m*ss s**gon play* will be her first professional production.

Helena Palmer CDG (Casting Director)

Helena Palmer CDG is a freelance casting director with over twenty years of experience. She began her casting career at the Royal Exchange, Manchester and then with the National Theatre. She was Casting Director at the RSC from 2008 to 2021, casting over fifty classical and contemporary plays. Projects include: *Beginning, Cat on a Hot Tin Roof, No Pay? No Way!* (Royal Exchange Theatre); *Cymbeline* (RSC); *The Tempest* (RSC); *Linck & Múlhahn, Mary* and *The Fever Syndrome* (Hampstead Theatre); *Dmitry* (Marylebone Theatre); *The Wind in the Willows, The Child in the Snow* (Wilton's Music Hall); *Sarah* (Coronet Theatre); *Blackmail, Antigone* (Mercury, Colchester); *The Mirror and the Light* (Gielgud Theatre).

Manchester's Royal Exchange Theatre Company transforms the way people see theatre, each other and the world around them. Our historic building was taken over by artists in 1976. Today it is an award-winning cultural charity that produces new theatre in-the-round, in communities, on the road and online.

Exchange remains at the heart of everything we make and do. Now our currency is brand new drama and reinvigorated classics, the boldest artists and a company of highly skilled makers – all brought together in a shared imaginative endeavour to trade ideas and experiences with the people of Greater Manchester (and beyond).

The Exchange's unique auditorium is powerfully democratic, a space where audiences and performers meet as equals, entering and exiting through the same doors. It is the inspiration for all we do; inviting everyone to understand the past, engage in today's big questions, collectively imagine a better future and lose themselves in the moment of a great night out.

The Royal Exchange was named Regional Theatre of the Year in 2016 and School of the Year at The Stage Awards 2018. Our work, developed with an incredible array of artists and theatre-makers, includes *Hamlet* with Maxine Peake (for stage and film), *The Skriker* (with the Manchester International Festival), *King Lear* (co-produced with Talawa Theatre Company, filmed for BBC iPlayer and BBC Four), *The House of Bernarda Alba* (a co-production with Graeae), *Light Falls* (a world-premiere from Simon Stephens, directed by Sarah Frankcom, with original music by Jarvis Cocker), *Wuthering Heights* (directed by Joint Artistic Director Bryony Shanahan), *Rockets and Blue Lights* (by award-winning writer Winsome Pinnock and directed by Miranda Cromwell), *Cat on a Hot Tin Roof*, *The Mountaintop* (Digital Streaming directed by Joint Artistic Director Roy Alexander Weise), *All I Want for Christmas* (digital commission for December 2020), *Bloody Elle – A Gig Musical* and *Let the Right One In* (directed by Bryony Shanahan).

Find out more on our website and social-media channels:

royalexchange.co.uk

@rxtheatre

Help us create extraordinary theatre on our stage and in our communities:

royalexchange.co.uk/support-us
or donations@royalexchange.co.uk

Donors and Supporters

Principal Funders

bruntwood

Corporate Partner
Bruntwood

Corporate Sponsor
Galloways Printers
Garratts Solicitors
Edwardian Hotels
Stock Exchange Hotel
Warner Bros. Discovery

Principle Corporate Member
Edmundson Electrical

Encore Corporate Member
Ralli Solicitors LLP
Slater Heelis
Torevell & Partners

Associate Corporate Member
5plus Architects
Beaverbrooks the Jewellers Ltd
HFL Building Solutions
Sanderson Weatherall

Our Trailblazers
Jason Austin
Ben & Becky Caldwell
Meg & Peter Cooper
John & Penny Early
Mike Edge & Pippa England
Richard & Elaine Johnson
Jack & Janice Livingstone
Carolyn & Andrew Mellor
Stuart Montgomery
Anthony Morrow & Family
Carole Nash OBE
Stephen & Judy Poster
Anthony & Margaret Preston
Nicola Shindler

Our Firelights
John Batley
Mr J Bishop & Mr J Taylor
Angela Brookes
Ron & Gillian Brown
Paul & Ann Cannings
Grace R Dutt, James Poole & Lena Poole
Mark Evans
Mrs V Fletcher
Nigel Gourlay
Irene Gray

Roy & Maria Greenwood
Geoff Holman
Stephen & Arlene Moss
Robin & Mary Taylor
Helen & Phil Wiles
Barry Harkison
Sir Robert and Dr Meriel Boyd

Our Campfire Members: £300
Daniel Bohuslaw
Gary Buttriss-Holt
Fiona Cooper
John & Kim Fox
George Hood
Patricia Kelly
Stella Lowe
Harriet Monkhouse
George Morton
JD & Sheila Rose
Mike Smith
Sebastian Taylor
Barry Williams

RXIGNITE Collective & Special Acknowledgments'
Arnold & Brenda Bradshaw
Barbara Crossley
Ellen Hanlon
Susan & Sally Hodgkiss CBE
Martyn & Valerie Torevell
The Baker Family Charitable Trust

Trusts And Foundations
The Backstage Trust
The Beaverbrooks Charitable Trust
The Esmée Fairbairn Foundation
The Granada Foundation
The Jigsaw Foundation
The John Lewis Partnership Golden Jubilee Trust
The Noël Coward Foundation
The Oglesby Charitable Trust
The Rayne Foundation
The Victoria Wood Foundation
Young Manchester

We would like to offer a special thank you to all of our donors who wish to remain anonymous

bruntwood

'The Bruntwood Prize International Award gave me the warmest welcome to the UK that I could ever have received. Being able to meet so many new people and have my work introduced to them through the Bruntwood process was an incredible gift that has led directly to one of the most beautiful collaborations I've ever had, working with director Roy Alexander Weise on the world premiere production of my play at the Royal Exchange.' *Kimber Lee*

A partnership between the Royal Exchange Theatre and property company Bruntwood, the Prize is an opportunity for writers of any background and experience to enter unperformed plays for the chance to win part of a prize fund totalling £40,000.

At the heart of the Bruntwood Prize for Playwriting is the principal that anyone and everyone can enter – it is entirely anonymous and scripts are judged purely on the basis of the work alone, with no knowledge of the identity of the playwright. Since its inception in 2005 over 15,000 scripts have been entered, £304,000 has been awarded to 34 prize-winning writers and 26 winning productions have been staged in 38 UK-wide venues.

Each winner enters into a development process with the Royal Exchange Theatre in an endeavour to bring their work to production. It is not guaranteed but we aspire to produce each play and find co-producers to give the plays a longer life and further reach. There have been co-productions with Lyric Hammersmith, Live Theatre, Soho Theatre, Bush Theatre, Orange Tree Theatre, Sherman Theatre, High Tide and the Royal Court Theatre. Work has also gone on to be produced internationally from Australia, USA, Germany, France, to Canada and Sweden. The Bruntwood Prize International Award was launched in 2019 and, through partnerships with theatres and organisations in Australia, Canada and the US, accepts submissions from playwrights.

The Bruntwood Prize for Playwriting is a genuine endeavour to discover new stories and help playwrights develop their craft, providing everybody and anybody with the opportunity to write a play. It offers a fantastic opportunity to hone your writing skills, whether or not you have written for the stage before.

More information can be found at **www.writeaplay.co.uk**

Factory International is the organisation behind Manchester International Festival (MIF) and a landmark new cultural space opening in 2023 – putting Manchester on the map as a world-leading destination for art.

With an ambitious year-round programme of original work, music and one-of-a-kind events, Factory International builds on the magic of MIF – and will continue to host the Festival every other year at its new home and venues across Greater Manchester.

Rooted in the city, Factory International creates space for the world's most exciting artists to invent tomorrow together, while supporting the next generation of local talent into the creative industries.

factoryinternational.org / @factoryintl / @factory_international

Factory International and MIF have a significant role to play in the UK's cultural economy and we are incredibly grateful for the support of our corporate and commercial partners, individual donors, trusts and foundations and public funders.

Principal Partner: Aviva
Official Partners: Bruntwood, Electricity North West, Selfridges
Hotel & Travel Partners: The Edwardian Manchester, Transport for Greater Manchester
Senior and Associate Supporters: BDP, Eversheds Sutherland, Hawkins\Brown, JLL, Manchester Metropolitan University, Mills & Reeve LLP, Regatta, The University of Manchester, Buro Happold, Civic Engineers, Landmark Group, Levitt Bernstein, Shoosmiths, Turley, Urban Splash, Williams BMW, Workshop Properties
Public Sector Funders: Manchester City Council, Arts Council England
Trusts & Foundations: Bloomberg Philanthropies, Esmée Fairbairn Foundation, Paul Hamlyn Foundation, The Granada Foundation, Law Family Charitable Foundation
Founding Cast: Beaverbrooks Charitable Trust, Garfield Weston Foundation, Law Family Charitable Foundation
Foundation Circle: The Black Family, Jo & Tom Bloxham MBE, Craig & Rita Hollingsworth, The Savannah Wisdom Foundation
Patrons & Pioneers: Jim Leaviss, Nick, Lucy & Owen Meikle-Williams, Simon Sack & Emma Almond, Lisa Ashurst, Matthew Claughton, Bob Gardner, Helen Gilman & Malcolm Pitcher, Laura Harper, Alice Rawsthorn, Andy Spinoza, Valerie & Martyn Torevell, John Williams

Factory International Staff

HUMAN RESOURCES
Ann-Marie Teed, HR Director. **Marney Guy,** Senior HR Advisor. **Sonia Watson-Fowler,** Equalities & Representation Manager. **Maddy Peden,** HR Coordinator. **Alex Derevianko,** Training Coordinator. **James Anderson,** Recruitment Administrator.

INTERNATIONAL
Paul Clay, International Director. **Eva Pepper,** Head of International Partnerships. **Michelle Rocha,** Head of Touring. **Hannah Falvey,** International Partnerships Manager. **Jasmine Skellern,** Production Administrator (International).

IT
Sean McErlean, Head of Venue IT. **Steven Bennett,** Deputy Head of Venue IT. **Bram Weston,** IT Coordinator. **Homer Lam, Zaw Oo,** IT Administrators.

MUSIC
Jane Beese, Director of Music.

PRODUCING
Kate Mackonochie, Director of Producing. **Seb Matthes,** Artist Liaison Manager. **Jessica Ambrose,** Festival Artist Liaison Manager. **Marcus Keane,** Ground Transport Coordinator. **Jami Bennett, Rachel Weston,** Artist Liaison Administrators. **Matthew Taylor,** Artist Liaison Assistant. **Fiona Pride,** Deputy Director of Producing. **Paul Elam,** Executive Producer. **Anna Moutrey, Ric Watts, Robert Croll, Ruhi Jhunjhunwala,** Senior Producers. **Catt Belcher, Katherine Wilde, Kwong Lee, Mai Komoriya, Pete Vance, Steve Vickers,** Producers. **Nina Franklin,** Producer (Digital & Broadcast). **Katie Bruce, Shaan Dua,** Event Managers. **Abi Hellam,** Producing Department Coordinator. **Rowan Lark,** Associate Producer. **Astarte Cara, Hester Cox, Laura Allan, Louis Lisle, Rebecca Burgess, Rosa Beuzeval,** Production Administrators. **Simaran Patel,** Producing Department Administrative Assistant. **Becky Shepherd,** Head of Scheduling & Producing Administration. **Ryan Coles,** Scheduler.

SUSTAINABILITY
Feimatta Conteh, Environmental Sustainability Manager.

SYSTEMS
David Fox, Head of Systems & Technology. **Mon Miah,** Deputy Head of Systems & Technology. **Emma Colledge,** Tech & Insights Project Officer. **Rajkumar Govindaraj,** Data Engineer.

TECHNICAL & FACILITIES
Paul Moore, Director of Production & Building Operations. **Jack Thompson,** Associate Technical Director. **John Gilleese,** Technical Manager. **Alex Adamson,** Head of Scenic & Gallery Installations. **David Wimpenny,** Head of Lighting & Video. **Sorcha Steele,** Head of Sound. **Dash Wong,** Deputy Head of Lighting. **James Unsworth,** Deputy Head of Exhibitions. **Tom French,** Deputy Head of Stage. **Rachael Lees,** Digital Production Manager. **Fraser Millward, Kelly Rossington-Otter, Lily Maketansky,** Technical Coordinators. **Ellis Robison, Joel Pendleton, Phil Thackray, Simon Beech, William Bower,** Sound Technicians. **David Mitchell,** Facilities Manager. **Simon Inkpen,** Deputy Facilities Manager. **Matt Ibbs, Ryan Clowes,** Facilities Management Technicians.

TICKETING
Marie Hirst, Head of Ticketing. **Joshua Lacey,** Ticketing Manager. **Josie Harrison,** Ticketing Coordinator. **Lerato Mokate,** Groups & Access Ticketing Coordinator. **Drew Forest, Lydia Bistucz, Tom Halls,** Ticketing Operations Supervisors. **James Webster,** Ticketing Administrator.

TRANSITION PROJECT
Nadia Balfe, Project Manager. **Marenka Vossen,** Project Officer (Transition). **Dean Meehan,** Venue Operations Programme Manager.

VISITOR EXPERIENCE
Rebecca Alexander, Head of Visitor Operations. **Joseph Daly,** Hospitality & Retail Operations Manager. **Laura Mina, Matthew Lane, Saeed Murtaza,** Front of House Managers.

VOLUNTEERING
Lee Ashworth, Volunteer Manager. **Esther Lisk-Carew,** Deputy Volunteer Manager. **Candice Hull,** Volunteer Assistant.

Young Vic

The Young Vic Theatre has been one of London's leading theatres for more than fifty years. It was founded in 1970 as a space for world-premiere productions as well as unexpected takes on classic plays that speak to our present.

Recent ground-breaking revivals include Simon Stone's *Yerma* starring Billie Piper, and Marianne Elliott and Miranda Cromwell's *Death of A Salesman* starring Wendell Pierce and Sharon D. Clarke. New critically acclaimed works first presented by the Young Vic include the multi-award-winning world premieres of Matthew Lopez's *The Inheritance* and James Graham's *Best of Enemies*.

Under the leadership of Artistic Director Kwame Kwei-Armah and Executive Director Lucy Davies, the Young Vic stands out in the city's cultural landscape for balancing daring commercial drive, artistic flair and success with genuine grassroots social impact.

For twenty-five years, we've put our local communities in Lambeth and Southwark at the heart of our theatre through our creative engagement program, Taking Part. Taking Part is the embodiment of the Young Vic spirit: that the arts are indispensable to a full life and that everyone should have the opportunity to participate. We work with young people, adults and schools, and engage with over 15,000 people a year, providing free tickets to all our shows and free creative and artistic opportunities to our participants.

The Young Vic Creators Program is the only scheme of its kind for multi- and anti-disciplinary artists. We offer artists and producers unique pathways to develop their craft through opportunities that range from skills-based workshops to trainee and assistant director roles and a two-year residency through the Genesis Fellow/Associate Director position. The Genesis Network provides an online community to over 2,000 artists and producers.

Artistic Director	**Kwame Kwei-Armah**
Executive Director	**Lucy Davies**

youngvic.org

Young Vic Theatre Staff

Artistic Director **Kwame Kwei-Armah**, Executive Director **Lucy Davies**, Associate Artistic Director **Sue Emmas**, Head of Artistic Development **Teunkie van der Sluijs**, Literary and Dramaturgy Associate **Olivia Poglio-Nwabali**, Young Associate – Artistic Development **Luna Sigle**, Head of Producing **Nisha Modhwadia**, Associate Producer **Holly Aston**, Producer **Christabel Holmes**, Assistant Producer (Maternity Leave) **Lucy Steward**, Assistant Producer (Maternity Cover) **Myles Sinclair**, Creators' Program Producer **Sandra Thompson-Quartey** Creators Program Administrator **Khánh Hạ Nguyễn**, Executive Assistant **Amy Cranston**, Channel 4 playwright **Lulu Raczka**,

Young Vic Artistic Associates
Glenn Davis, Alfred Enoch, Anna Fleischle, Marcus Gardley, Kate Hewitt, Afua Hirsch, Kirsty Housley, Alex Basco Koch, Doña Kroll, Gregory Maqoma, Prema Mehta, Duncan McLean, Chinonyerem Odimba, Wendell Pierce, Caitriona Shoobridge, Charles Randolph-Wright, Charlotte Sutton, XANA

DEVELOPMENT
Development Director **Pippa Moore**, Senior Development Manager **Ama Ofori-Darko**, Development Co-ordinator **Emily Hamilton**

FINANCE
Finance Director **Cath Longman-Jones**, Finance Manager (Maternity Leave) **Janine Carter**, Finance Manager (Maternity Cover) **Orla Sanders**, Finance Assistant **Amy Morbin**

MARKETING & AUDIENCES
Director of Marketing and Audiences **Beatrice Burrows**, Head of Press and Communications **Su-Ann Chow-Seegoolam**, Senior Marketing Manager **Steph Cullen**, Senior Ticketing and Sales Manager **Zoe Fitzpatrick**, Social Media and Digital Content Manager **Florence Bell**, Press Officer **Karl-Lydie Jean-Baptiste**, Digital Marketing and Communications Officer **Aimee Dickinson**

OPERATIONS
Operations Director **Rathi Kumar**, Head of Systems and Technology **Fi Joseph**, Digital Systems Analyst **Damilola Senbanjo**

Head of People **Maria Khan**, Administrator **Sophie Byatt**, Head of Theatre Operations **Bryan Lewis**, Facilities Assistant **Chiara Ciabattoni**, Front of House and Welcome Team Manager **Ryan Mellish**, Assistant Front of House Manager **Eleanor Kumar**, Assistant Welcome Team Manager **Max Puplett**

Ushers
Aisha Edwards, Albert Graver, Andre Da Silva-Jenkins, Anna-May Wood, Ayisha Mi, Benjamin Clarke, Cassiopeia Berkeley-Agyepong, Charlie Cuscito, Charlotte Micalef, Chenta Mariqueo, Ciaran Cross, Daniella Randall, Debbie Burningham, Dynzell Muguti, Eboni Dixon, Ellis Jupiter, Grace Kayibanda, Gracjana Rejmer-Canovas, Grainne PC, Hana Jennings, Isaac Vincent, Jade Causton, Jida Akil, Joanna Selcott, Josh Hitchman-Pinnock, Joyce Clark, Julie Patten, Kitti Wells, Lethaniel Stacey-Coombe, Liam Thorley, Linden Sloan, Luke Garner-Greene, Lynn Knight, Malika SandoverMatheus Vianna, Maurice Chung, Max Pawley, Melina Barnett, Michael Asiamah, Millie Whittam, Molly-Rose Curran, Oliver Byng, Owen Haslegrave, Paula Shaw, Sahana Rackal, Sharitah Boulton, Simone Bell, Starr Ballard, Tanjiana Bryan-Hesse, Taz Munyaneza, Tom Sparkes
Duty Managers **Lauren Holden, Sebastian Houillon**

PRODUCTION
Technical Director **Craig Tye**, Head of Sound **Kyle MacPherson**, Head of Stage **Rhodri Evans**, Head of Costume (Maternity Leave) **Sarah Hamza**, Head of Costume (Maternity Cover) **Olivia Ward**, Head of Lighting **Faye Hetherington**, Deputy Head of Sound **Neil McKeown**, Deputy Head of Stage **Aaron Storey**, Deputy Head of Costume **Aimee Russam**, Workshop Manager **Rachel MacLoughlin**, Lighting Technician **Luke Jackson**, Stage Technician **Emma Horne** Production Administrator **Mengfei Liu** Young Associate – Production **Audrey Owusu-Frempong**

TAKING PART
Director of Taking Part **Shereen Jasmin Phillips**, Neighbourhood Theatre Producer **Alisha Artry**, Participation Producer **Aaliyah Antoine**, Learning Producer **Melanie Anouf**, Taking Part Administrator **Michelle Cullimore**

Young Associates – Taking Part and Creators Program **Alicia Pope, Elina Oliva Romo**

WELCOME TEAM
Edward Jones, Emily McCredie, Gracjana Rejmer-Canovas, Joel Oladapo, Julie Patten, Kathy Bolt, Lethaniel Stacey-Coombe, Mairin Schmidt, Sarah Baiden, Tia Harding, Tia Wingate

Headlong

We're Headlong.

We make theatre with the power to move.

Big, exhilarating productions that use the unexpected to connect everyone we reach, right across the nation.

Whether a work is old or new, there are always different questions we can ask.

So our productions are an invitation: to come and see something in a new way. Join us.

Previous Headlong productions include *Henry V*, *Jitney*, *Corrina, Corrina*, *Best of Enemies*, *People, Places & Things*, *The Nether*, *1984* and *Enron*, and major digital theatre innovations *Signal Fires* and *Unprecedented*.

Artistic Director   **Holly Race Roughan**
Executive Director   **Lisa Maguire**

For Headlong

General Manager **Joni Carter**
Marketing Manager **Bella Cox**
Development Manager **Lucy Howard-Taylor**
Finance Director **Keerthi Kollimada**
Executive Director **Lisa Maguire**
Assistant Producer **Radha Mamidipudi**
Executive Assistant **Carla-Marie Metcalfe**
Development Consultant **Kirstin Peltonen**
Literary Manager **Frank Peschier**
Producer **Zoë Anjuli Robinson**
Artistic Director **Holly Race Roughan**
Communities Associate **Iskandar إسكندر R. Sharazuddin**
Artist/Designer in Residence **Moi Tran**

Our Supporters
Headlong is grateful for the generous support of the following Trusts and Foundations:
Backstage Trust
The Buffini Chao Foundation
Noël Coward Foundation

We would like to thank the following individuals and companies for their generous support:
Neil and Sarah Brener
Annabel Duncan-Smith & Victoria Leggett
Alyce Faye Eichelberger-Cleese
Nick Hern Books
Jack and Linda Keenan
Beth and Ian Mill KC
Rob O'Rahilly

We are also grateful for the dedicated support of our Board members:
Justin Audibert, Kathy Bourne (Chair), Anna Cornelius, Paddy Dillon, Cas Donald, Sarah Ellis, Lucinda Harvey, Julia Head, Claire Heaney, Jacqueline Hurt, Prime Isaac, Lil Lambley, Sir Trevor Phillips OBE, Toni Racklin, Lesley Wan

Supported using public funding by
ARTS COUNCIL ENGLAND

untitled fuck miss saigon play
(srsly, this is not the title)
(oh well)

kimber lee

untitled fuck miss saigon play was first written and developed with the support of the Lark Play Development Center in NYC in 2017 and in 2018 the Ground Floor at Berkeley Repertory Theatre.

The play was also developed during a residency at the Eugene O'Neill Theater Center's National Playwrights Conference in 2019. (Wendy Goldberg, Artistic Director; Preston Whiteway, Executive Director.)

The play also received a workshop at the 2019 Ojai Playwrights Conference.

Acknowledgements

A play passes through so many hands while making its way in the world, and I'm forever grateful for the many brilliant and dedicated artists who have had a part in bringing this story to its fullest life on stage.

To all of the actors, directors, stage managers, dramaturgs and fellow playwrights who have given of themselves to support the journey: you have held the beating heart of this play with such care, generosity, hilarity and faith – thank you with all my heart for everything you have given. With special thanks to Tiffany Villarin, Jackie Chung, and everyone at the Lark who read pages for me.

Thank you to everyone at the 2018 Ground Floor at Berkeley Rep and especially Madeleine Oldham, the team at the 2019 O'Neill National Playwrights Conference, the 2019 Ojai Playwrights Conference, and the readers and Judges of the 2019 Bruntwood Prize. Thank you to Manchester International Festival, Headlong Theatre, the Young Vic, and the team at the Royal Exchange Theatre, especially Suzanne Bell and Chloe Smith.

To Roy Alexander Weise, all my love and gratitude for your one-of-a-kind heart, unfailing advocacy, unmatched sense of humor, and incomparable artistry: this could not have happened here with anyone but you. Thank you for your faith in me and the play. I will buy you something at the Wait-rose.

To Lloyd Suh, Andrea Hiebler, Krista Williams: I don't know if you realize how much your support and love and insight and fierce kindness mean to the many playwrights who have been lucky enough to know you. I will never stop being grateful to you for everything you do for me as a person and as a playwright, so stop squirming and just accept the love.

And for Haze: thank you. For it all. I'll be home soon.

Love always,
Kimber

Royal Exchange Theatre, Manchester
31 May 2023

'It is particularly sad and ironic that this controversy should surround a piece of theatre such as *Miss Saigon*, a tragic love story in which a young woman sacrifices her life to ensure that her Amerasian son may find a better life in America.'

Cameron Mackintosh

'Some people who are irritated by these criticisms of *Miss Saigon*'s enduring popularity will say, It's only a show, nothing more.

But the enjoyment of the show's fantasy is precisely why the show matters. Fantasy cannot be dismissed as mere entertainment, especially when we keep repeating the fantasy…

Racism and sexism are not incompatible with art… Our enjoyment of a work of art does not mean that the work cannot be racist or sexist, or that our enjoyment does not come from a deep-seated well of derogatory images of Asians and Asian women.

The unsettling paradox here is that we can indeed love and desire people whom we see in completely racist and sexist ways. That is the real, unintended universal truth of *Miss Saigon*.'

Viet Thanh Nguyen

Characters

KIM, *female. Asian American. Early twenties* (*or can pass for early twenties*)
ROSIE/CIO-CIO, *female. Asian American. Forties–fifties* (*or can pass for forties–fifties*)
AFI/GORO, *male. Asian American. Twenties–thirties*
CLARK, *male. White. Twenties–early thirties*
EVELYN/RICHARDS, *female. White. Twenties–early thirties*
NARRATOR/BRENDA, *female. Actor of color. Thirties*

And THE BAND. *Is there a live band? Maybe.*

Note on Text

Stage directions in parentheses are not read aloud.

Actually anything in parentheses is not read aloud, though the NARRATOR will read all stage directions that are not in parentheses.

The NARRATOR speaks through a microphone.

Translations in square brackets can be projected as subtitles, or spoken by the NARRATOR, or both.

This text went to press before the end of rehearsals and so may differ slightly from the play as performed.

1906

Date of the NYC premiere of Puccini's opera, third draft,
Madama Butterfly *at the Metropolitan Opera.*

NARRATOR (*on a mic*). Lights up on a muddy road through
a muddy village, which, though muddy, is also misty and
mysterious.

There's music – a swelling overture of some kinda vaguely
shakuhachi/shamisen type of thing with a Western vibe laid
over the top for dramatic tension.

Peasants shuffle to and fro, some might have baskets on their
heads; they gesticulate, like peasants do.

KIM enters, she is young, virginal, frightened, plucky,
hopeful, noble, dirt poor but very clean otherwise, and has
really great skin.

A massive horn blast from a steamship arriving in the nearby
harbor shakes the air.

The peasants gape at the sky in awe and exclaim
unintelligibly: (*Like maybe they just mutter the same word
over and over, like 'ohayo gozaimasu' for instance.*)

Another blast from the ship (*closer, louder*) the peasants
exclaim and scurry.

KIM tries to scurry, takes one step, and falls down.

KIM. Oh!

NARRATOR. ROSIE enters, an older peasant woman wearing
the standard Asian peasant pajama set but with a Western
vest over the top and a pair of bright-red cowboy boots.

(*She drags* KIM *to her feet.*)

ROSIE. Kim!! The Americans are here! It's our chance to
escape this cesspool of a country!

KIM. What?

ROSIE. Don't you want to go to America?

KIM. Uh –

ROSIE. It's our only hope!

KIM. Oh my god! Really? But I don't have any money for a ticket!

NARRATOR. ROSIE slaps KIM's ass.

ROSIE. That's your ticket right there, my little cherry blossom!

KIM (*shy, embarrassed*). Oh, Mother!

ROSIE. Just follow my lead and we'll wave sayonara to this shitstain of a village and be on our way to a new life in America where there are equal rights for women!
Stand up straight, shoulders back, tits up – here comes your future!

NARRATOR. (*They stand at the side of the road.*) ROSIE arranges KIM's clothes and hair for the sexiest effect.

KIM stands quietly, like a doll being dressed.

(*Lights shift*), a romantic haze floods the stage as:

CLARK enters.

He is tall, he is boyish and rugged and handsome and clearly does weights, cardio and High Intensity Interval Training at least four times a week – he looks like he could lift KIM up and break her in half over his knee, but he also exudes a very attractive manly gentleness and social-consciousness which we can discern in the way he regards with revulsion the oily conniving peasant men scurrying around him, trying to sell him their daughters.
The scurrying peasants part like the sea as CLARK strides through the village.

(*Text in square brackets should be projected as subtitles, or spoken by* NARRATOR, *or both.*)

CLARK. Maki. [Greetings.]
>Kimono sushi ohayo ichi ni san. [We come in peace from the West.]
>Maguro! Saba! [We bring news of the modern world to you!]
>Kyoto dojo katana – [We hope to open trade and avert any conflict with –]

NARRATOR. His eyes meet KIM's across the scurrying crowd. She lowers her eyes modestly, ROSIE grins and pulls her over to CLARK.

ROSIE. Welcome to our humble village, most Number One American Son.

CLARK. Onigiri. Sake. Hashi…? [Thanks. I'm happy to be here. And this is…?]

ROSIE. This is Kim.
>Would you like to come over for dinner?

CLARK. Honto go! [Would I ever!]
>Okonomiyaki. [Say eight?]

ROSIE. Maybe earlier – at six?

CLARK. Kurosawa. [Wonderful.]

NARRATOR. He gently lifts KIM's chin, her eyes flutter shyly.

CLARK. Fujisan momotaro. [I can't wait.]

NARRATOR. He bows over her hand, kissing it respectfully yet also kinda sexy-sexy like.
>KIM's eyes go wide, she's never felt man-lips on her skin and it awakens something inside her… something *sexy* like.

>(CLARK *smiles and strides away, the villagers murmuring around him*.)

KIM (*holding the hand* CLARK *kissed*). What is happening?

NARRATOR. ROSIE cackles (*delighted*) whips out a shamisen and plays an upbeat song as the scene shifts – maybe something like 'Proud Mary', the Tina Turner version but with a shamisen.

ROSIE. You are my golden ticket, girlie –

KIM. What? But…

ROSIE. – the way out of this stinking mudhole!
I mean do you really want to stay in this hut for the rest of
your life?

KIM. Uh –

ROSIE. What other possible future is there for you?

KIM. I had so many dreams.

ROSIE. Psshh – what dreams? You can't eat dreams.

KIM. Well, but there was that one about having some kind of
rice delivery business, I was going to call it 'Rice Now'
but… but then the rice famine happened and the investors
pulled out, so…

ROSIE. So… no dreams.

KIM. Goro the fishmonger's son has offered to marry me.

ROSIE. Goro the fishmonger's son is not a dream.

KIM. He likes my rice delivery idea. He was gonna do a fish
side to go with it: 'Rice Now, Fish Later'.

ROSIE. Listen to your mama, you foolish girl. You gotta learn
how to defer gratification. If you do your duty, you will have
a rice delivery *empire* in America. And fishmongery? Really?
Nothing gets that stink off you at the end of the day, trust me.

NARRATOR. GORO scurries past with a giant basket of fish on
his head, leaving a strong smell of fish in his wake.

GORO. Hey Kim!

KIM. Hey Goro!

GORO. The mackerel are running today! I'll save one for ya!

ROSIE. Kim. My girl. Be better than Goro the fishmonger's
son. Be better than all of this.

KIM. I mean…

ROSIE. Why have the gods made you so beautiful? For nothing?

KIM. I mean –

ROSIE. It's so you can go to America! Shake that tight ass and
we will rise up from the mud and fishy smell of this place!

NARRATOR. (KIM *looks at her hand where* CLARK *kissed it*.)
A waft of romantic CLARK-haze across the stage, KIM
looks off into the distance, bravely.

KIM. Very well. I will do what I must do, Mother.

ROSIE. Great, now go take a bath. And be sure you get
everything clean.

KIM (*shy, embarrassed*). Mother!

ROSIE. You never know where the night will take you, it's best
to be prepared. I left some cherry blossom soap by the tub
and we don't have a razor but I gave my fish knife a good
going over with Kenji's sharpening stone, so, you know...
be thorough.

NARRATOR. KIM bows, exits.
ROSIE cackles and plays the shamisen again, perhaps
'Celebration' by Kool and The Gang.

(*She sings and whoever is helping with the set change sings
along*.)

DANCE BREAK.

Happy villagers, happy in their simple village way.

ROSIE *and others*. Ceee-leh-brate good times come on!
duh nuh nuh nuh, nuh nuh, nuh nuh...

(ROSIE *and the others continue to sing the first refrain and
verse of 'Celebration'*.)

Meanwhile, a tiny hut-like dwelling has emerged...

So the interior of the hut is Asian in the sense that there is
probably a lot of bamboo that has been distressed with a
dark-brown stain to make a properly dark, mysterious locale;
might be some noren curtains in the doorway, printed with
bamboo patterns; cushions on the floor (*no chairs*) a low
table, lots of oil lamps and candles.

Maybe the whole place looks like Pier 1 and Cost Plus had
a three-way with Ikea and this hut is their bastard mixed-race
child.

(ROSIE *fluffs up a futon bed nearby, exits*.)

(*Lights shift to*) evening, after dinner.

CLARK, KIM, and ROSIE sit around the low table, sipping
after-dinner tea.
KIM is decked out in full kimono with her hair done up high
and tight, full of flowers and sparkly ornaments.
CLARK can't keep his eyes off her, she keeps her eyes
modestly lowered.

CLARK. Furikake. [Your hair looks really nice.]

NARRATOR. KIM covers her mouth and smiles, with a little
shy shake of her head.
ROSIE brings a plate of mochi to the table (*grins*) offers
a gold paper crown to CLARK.

CLARK. Desho? [What's this?]

ROSIE (*sneaky grin*). Dessert hat.

CLARK. Sashimi! [How fun!]

NARRATOR. ROSIE puts a golden cloth on KIM's head, hands
them each a mochi, directs them to feed a bite to each other,
which they do.

ROSIE. And I now pronounce you...
(*Whispers*.)... husband and wife!

CLARK. Tataki? [What was that?]

ROSIE. Mochi is yummy!

CLARK. Ah, dojo, dojo! [Yes, it is!]

(ROSIE *stretches and yawns elaborately*.)

ROSIE. Welp! I'm all tuckered out, I think I'll turn in. Enjoy
your mochi, kids.

CLARK. Daiko, Rosie. [Thank you, Rosie.]
Yamamoto. [Goodnight.]

NARRATOR. ROSIE leaves, but we see her eyes peeking through the bamboo wall.

CLARK inches closer to KIM, who brings out a fan and hides her face shyly.

CLARK. Pachinko. [Don't be afraid.]

KIM. Oh… hee-hee.

CLARK. Kim.

KIM. Yes?

CLARK (*savoring her name on his tongue like a fine port wine*). Kiiiiiiiimmmmmm… KimKimKim…

KIM.…yes?

CLARK (*points at himself*). Clark Jackson Lincoln Garfield.

KIM. Coo-lah-rak… Jehck-uh-som-rinkuh… Guh-rah-ruh-feeduh.

(*He laughs, charmed.*)

CLARK. Sakura tatami obi. [You have captured me with your maiden's heart.]

KIM. Okay.

CLARK. Shohei ohtani. [Look at me.]

NARRATOR. She meets his gaze shyly, he gently touches her cheek.

CLARK. O-bun furoshiki. [You are like the moon and stars.]

KIM (*fluttery, flattered*). Ohhh…

NARRATOR. Her eyes flutter bashfully, he grasps her chin. They gaze at each other, the sexual tension building.

CLARK. Gomi leah nanako, tabi yo, hayao miyazaki. [You fill the sky, my sky, your silvery light.]

KIM. And you are the sun, warming me with your kind, round American eyes, and your – wow, you are really the largest man I've ever seen up close, your chest, your arms, your –

NARRATOR. He presses his man parts onto her lady parts.

KIM. – whoa.

NARRATOR. He kisses her passionately, her shyness seems to have worn off because *dayum* – she's a natural at the exotic sexy-sexy stuff.

CLARK. You taste like moonlight and jasmine and mystery!

KIM. You taste like freedom!

NARRATOR. They make out, rolling around on the cushions – (*At one point she thumps at his arm, he stops, she pants heavily.*)

KIM. Sorry. Couldn't breathe there for a second.

CLARK. Yes this feeling is so powerful –

KIM. – no your arm was on my windpipe. Anyway. Carry on.

NARRATOR. More making out, he stands with her in his arms like she is a twig, carries her to the futon where they continue to get it on.

(*Lights dim, and*) ROSIE pulls down a curtain around the bed.
She whips out her shamisen and plays a slow-jam version of 'The Rhythm of the Night' by DeBarge.
(*Lights fade to black.*)
An inexplicably and overwhelmingly loud, long blast from the steamship's horn – is there something orgasmic about it? Maybe.

Peasants scurry around the stage, changing the scene to:

Four Years Later.

The hut has not aged well, the noren curtain hangs in shreds, the walls are just flat-out busted, one pale lamp burns on the low table near a large photo of ROSIE, who has died.

KIM stands gazing out the window toward the harbor.
She is still pretty but her Asian pajamas are very raggedy, her hair is unkempt, and her face is smudged with grime like she

works at a Jiffy Lube auto-repair shop.
Also she has a runny nose.
Another blast from a ship.

KIM. Oh! He has come back! I see his ship glide into the harbor
like a swan or maybe a crane! At last, he has come back for
us as he promised!

NARRATOR. She hugs ROSIE's photo.

KIM. At last, Mother! I will fulfill your dreams!
I must take a bath!

NARRATOR. She wipes her nose and runs offstage.

CLARK enters, stands outside the hut with EVELYN, his
white American wife.

CLARK. You are the best, most noble woman I know, Evelyn.

EVELYN. Oh, Clark.

CLARK. How many other wives would stand by their husbands
after learning of his terrible, dark past?

EVELYN. How could I abandon you to the nightmarish burden
you have carried these past four years?

CLARK. You have saved me from my dark memories, Evelyn.
They are so dark. So oily and greasy and dark –

EVELYN. I know. Let's say no more about it, darling. We must
do what we must do.
We will take the child and never return to this place.

CLARK. Yes, but I –

NARRATOR. (*He breaks off as*) KIM runs in, hair wet from her
bath.

KIM. My love, I knew you would not forget me!

(*She stops short when she sees* EVELYN.)

Wait, who is this?
Who is she?
Who are you?

EVELYN (*to* CLARK). Well.
  She's every bit as pretty as you said.

CLARK. Kim, shogun origami. [Kim, it's been a long time. You
  look well.]
  Edamame, Evelyn. [This is my wife, Evelyn.]

KIM. Your *wife*?

NARRATOR. CLARK nods, EVELYN holds up her ring hand.
  KIM falls to her knees.

KIM. But… *I'm* your wife.

NARRATOR. She runs to the hut and brings out the gold paper
  crown, now a little worse for wear.

  (CLARK *looks puzzled*.)

KIM. Don't you remember? Rosie brought us the wedding
  mochi?

CLARK. Where is Rosie anyway, I –
  Oh wait. Oh no. Oh wow.
  Are you telling me that was… wasabi shoyu? [A wedding?]

KIM. Yes, a wedding.
  And Rosie died.

CLARK. Tamago. [I'm so sorry.]

EVELYN. Clark, what's going on? You know I don't speak her
  language.
  Did she say she's… your wife?

CLARK. No no no no! Of course not! *You* are my only wife,
  Evelyn –

  (KIM *gives an anguished little cry and falls to her knees
  again*.)

  – what happened with Kim was – you know, there were all
  these trade deadlines and treaties – everything was passing
  before my eyes –

KIM. Passing!

CLARK. When I got back home, it was like I woke from a bad dream and there you were –

KIM. Bad dream!

CLARK. You saved me from myself!

EVELYN (*touched by his declaration*). Oh, Clark!

KIM (*despairing*). Oh, Clark!

NARRATOR. CLARK and EVELYN embrace, make out a little.
The kissing goes on maybe a tad longer than is really comfortable for everyone.
KIM (*watches them*) moans a little in despair, then she resigns herself, walks tragically into the hut, and returns with a child – which may be played by a very large doll dressed as a peasant child. (*But even if you use a real child, he or she should never move or show emotion, the others should pick him or her up and use him or her like a prop.*)

CLARK and EVELYN stare at the child.

(**KIM** *prostrates herself before them.*)

KIM. Please, I beg of you! Take my son with you to America!

(*Pause.*)

Please! He must have the life I am unable to give him! Take him away from the dirt and the grime and the greasy fish oils of this place! I am begging you please please –

EVELYN. Okay.

KIM. – what?

EVELYN. We'll take him.

NARRATOR. Evelyn holds out her arms, the child runs to her, she scoops him up.

EVELYN. See you back at the ship, darling.
Don't dawdle.

(*She exits.*)

NARRATOR. KIM weeps on the ground, CLARK pats her head awkwardly.

CLARK. Tamago. [I'm sorry.]
Tam, tam, tamago. [I'm so, so sorry.]

KIM. You will give him everything I wanted for him? He will have the world?

CLARK. Haribo! [Yes!]

KIM. Then go! Leave me!

NARRATOR. He reaches for her, she turns her face away from him
He pats her hair and leaves.
KIM drags herself to her feet, wipes her runny nose on her sleeve like the peasant she is, goes into the hut.
The candle by ROSIE's photo has burned low, flickering.
KIM pulls ROSIE's fish knife from under the futon.
She presses the point against her chest, then stomach, then her temple, between her chest and stomach – trying to find the best place, she's never done this before.
She sighs, hums a little vaguely Asian lullaby (*then says*):

KIM (*soft, tragic, noble*). You were my sun, now our son is your sun.
The moon is down.

NARRATOR. And then suddenly, she slices herself across the throat in one quick move,
SHNICK,
and slumps over, very gracefully, her hair spreading on the floor very poetically, her hand extended open with the knife fallen on the floor in a perfect line pointing to ROSIE's picture.
The candle sputters and goes out.

Blackout.

1949

(*Date of the Broadway premiere of* South Pacific.)

NARRATOR. A muddy little village on a muddy little island
somewhere in the South Pacific.
A sweaty marketplace, island people scurrying to and fro,
some with baskets on their head.
KIM enters carrying some mangoes on her head – young,
virginal, frightened, hopeful, et cetera.
Sounds of a war plane passing overhead.
The island people look skyward, muttering in some vaguely
Polynesian way (*like 'lani kai' and 'pahoa'*).

A muffled but very deep boom from the direction the plane
went in – the villagers (*'oooh' and 'aahhhh' and*) point to the
sky in wonder.

Another, louder boom – the villagers cringe, cry out, and
scurry around
KIM falls down, her mangoes go flying, she crawls around
picking them out of the mud.
A man named AFI runs on, pulls KIM to her feet.

AFI. The Americans are here!

KIM. Ouch, my mangoes –

AFI. It's our chance to escape this cesspool of an island!

KIM. Uh –

AFI. We can start over in America!

KIM. But Afi, I don't have any money for a ticket! You spent
the dowry my father gave you for our wedding on drinking
and gambling and trying to corner the pineapple market!

NARRATOR. AFI slaps KIM's ass.

AFI. That's your ticket right there, my little hibiscus flower!
I knew that ass would be gold one day. Don't you want
a new life in America where there are equal rights for all
men regardless of skin color?
Stand up straight, shoulders back, tits up – don't mess this up
for me or I'll make you pay.

NARRATOR. They stand at the side of the road, AFI pushes
    KIM forward.
    (*Lights shift*), a romantic haze floods the stage as:
    CLARK enters with RICHARDS, another soldier.
    CLARK is tall/boyish/rugged/handsome, does
    weights/cardio/Interval Training, et cetera, et cetera.
    Scurrying peasants part like a field of grasses, and sound like
    one too since they are all wearing grass skirts (*as* CLARK
    strides through the village).

CLARK. Katsu. [Greetings.]
    Lau lau lychee tako. [We parked our planes in your
    sugarcane fields.]
    Puu-puu saimin. [Don't tell anyone.]
    Hanalei kona – [We stopped by for lunch and a strategic
    foothold in the Pacific theater –]

NARRATOR. RICHARDS puts the moves on a peasant girl.

RICHARDS. Well, well – lookee what we have here…

    (CLARK *grabs his arm.*)

CLARK. Richards!

RICHARDS. Aw, come on, Clark – just a little harmless R&R!

CLARK. For god's sake, man! You don't treat these people like
    that!
    (*To the girl.*) Kahlua. [Sorry about that.]

NARRATOR. CLARK looks up and sees KIM, their eyes lock.
    Heat crackles between them.
    AFI grins and pulls her toward CLARK.
    She resists weakly.
    AFI slaps her butt, she cries out.
    CLARK strides over to them.

CLARK. Lani kai! [Leave her alone!]

AFI. Welcome to our humble village, most Best Quality
    American GI.

CLARK. Waikiki. Lei. Poke…? [Thanks. I'm happy to be here.
    And this is…?]

AFI. This is Kim, my… sister.

KIM. That's not tr–

(AFI *elbows her in the ribs*.)

– ow –

AFI. Would you like to come over for dinner?

CLARK. Ono! [Would I ever!]
Lolo leelo? [Say eight?]

AFI. Perfect!
Here's the address.

NARRATOR. AFI gives him a ti leaf with directions written on it.

(CLARK *looks at* KIM *again, nods and smiles, her eyes flutter shyly*.)

CLARK. Maui manoa. [I can't wait.]

NARRATOR. He bows, does sexy-sexy hand kissing, exits.
KIM's eyes go wide from sexy man-lips, et cetera.

KIM. What is happening…?

She looks at her hand where CLARK kissed it, rubs it against her face (*and then there's a split second of déjà vu: 'wait a minute…'*)

(*She shrugs it off*.)

NARRATOR. AFI (*laughs*) whips out a ukelele and plays an upbeat song as the scene shifts – maybe something like ukelele 'I Feel For You' by Chaka Khan.

AFI. You're our golden ticket to the future, baby!

KIM. But isn't it weird that I'm engaged to you but you want me to go with him…?
That doesn't make you feel weird?

AFI. No. Why would it?

(*Beat*.)

KIM. Yeah I still think it's kinda –

NARRATOR. AFI smacks her across the face, she goes flying.

KIM. Oof!

AFI. Don't you want to eat something besides papaya?

KIM. But what about my dreams –

AFI. Oh my god –

NARRATOR. He smacks her again.

KIM. Owf…!

AFI. Stop being crazy! You don't got any dreams!

KIM. Well there was my idea for a mushed-up fruit and ice stand, where we'd mush up fruit and ice and call it 'mushie' sell it to the field laborers, but then we could never figure out where all that ice would come from since refrigeration is such an issue…

AFI. I'm supposed to smack you again but this humidity is really getting to me...

(*She looks at him, they both look around suddenly – a moment of awareness…? – then back to –*)

KIM. Goro the fishmonger's son has offered to marry me if you don't want to.

AFI. Goro the fishmonger's son. Seriously. You really just said that to me.

KIM. He likes my mushie idea. He was gonna do a fish side to go with it: 'Mushie and Sushi'.

AFI. Listen to me, dummy. If we go to America, you can have anything you want! You don't have to grow old bearing the children of a man who thinks fish oil is hair care!

KIM. Fish oil has many health benefits —

AFI. Come on, Kim! Be better than Goro the fishmonger's son, can't you? Be better than all of this, all of these greasy, sweating, mongoose villagers just putting one foot in front of the other for the rest of their greasy mongoose lives.

KIM. I used to have a pet mongoose named Buboy. He was so loyal.

AFI. All right fine, fuck it – if you won't dream for yourself, can't you just help me get my dream? Huh? What about *my* dreams?? You don't wanna marry me, fine – but at least don't bogart my American dream with your selfish, puritanical ways! If you wanna stay in a place where you gotta hide your gifts under a fishwife's muumuu that's fine but you don't gotta drag me down too! Let me live, Kim!! LET ME LIVE!!

(*Beat:* KIM *shrugs.*)

KIM. Okay.

AFI. Great, now go make me a fish sandwich and then take a bath.
And be sure you wash *everything*, I hear these American GIs like a clean, well-lit workspace.

KIM (*giggly, embarrassed*). Afi!

AFI. You never know where the night will take you, it's best to be prepared.
I left some hibiscus and gardenia soap by the tub and we don't have a razor but I gave my abalone knife a good going over with Kenji's sharpening stone, so, you know… be thorough.

(KIM *bows, exits.*)

NARRATOR. AFI cackles and starts playing the uke again, perhaps a slow-jam version of 'Give It To Me Baby' by Rick James.
Meanwhile, our tiny Pier 1-love-child, hut-like dwelling has emerged…

(*Lights shift to*) later in the evening, after dinner.
CLARK and KIM at the low table, sipping after dinner rum drinks with tiny umbrellas.
KIM is decked out in full muumuu/hula dancer costume with her hair cascading over her shoulders, full of flowers.

CLARK can't keep his eyes off her but she keeps her eyes
modestly lowered.
AFI brings a plate of sliced mango to the table, glances back
and forth between them.
He offers a crown of hibiscus flowers to CLARK.

CLARK. Hana? [What's this?]

AFI. Dessert hat.
Island custom.

CLARK. Pali! [Wonderful!]

NARRATOR. AFI puts a chain of flowers around KIM's neck,
hands them each a slice of mango, directs them to offer a bite
to each other, which they do.

AFI. And I now pronounce you… mananwife!

CLARK. Kamehameha? [What was that?]

AFI. Mango is yummy!

CLARK. Ala moana! [Yes, it is!]

(AFI *stretches and yawns elaborately*.)

AFI. Welp! Past my bedtime!

KIM. Afi…

CLARK. Malasadas, Afi. [Thank you, Afi.]
Ono. [Goodnight.]

NARRATOR. AFI leaves, but we see his eyes peeking through
the bamboo wall.
CLARK inches closer to KIM, who brings out a palm frond
and hides her face shyly.

(*At certain moments, a very, <u>very slight</u> edge of impatience
creeps into* KIM'*s voice though she quickly goes back to
smiling, sweet and shy.*)

CLARK. Kama maka mooka. [Don't be afraid.]

KIM. I'm not.
And those aren't actually words you just said.

CLARK. Kim.

KIM. Yes…?

CLARK (*savoring her name on his tongue like a fine port wine*). Kiiiiiiimimimim…

KIM. Mmhm, that's my name.

CLARK (*points at himself*). Clark Jackson Lincoln Garfield.

KIM. Clak… Jahck-som-rinkoo Gahffd.

(*He laughs, charmed.*)

CLARK. Hana hana ono kelikimaka. [You have captured me with your maiden's heart.]

KIM. Okay.

CLARK. Hapa. [Look at me.]

NARRATOR. (*She meets his gaze shyly, he gently touches her cheek.*) His touch sets her on fire.

CLARK. Hulihuli loon. [You are like the moon.]

KIM (*fluttery, flattered*). Woooowww, I feel so… no man has ever made me feel the way you make me feel… you're so tall and… wide and… big…

NARRATOR. Her eyes flutter bashfully – (*he grasps her chin*) et cetera.
They gaze at each other (*the sexual tension building*), et cetera.

CLARK. Mahi mahi, hana, loon. [You fill the sky, my sky, your silvery light.]

KIM. And you are the sun, warming me with your big American (eyes) –

NARRATOR. He leans in and kisses her, they make out, sexy futon time, et cetera, et cetera.
(*Fade to black as*) a warplane engine roars to life, in a slightly orgasmic kinda way? Maybe.

Four Years Later.

In the busted-ass hut one pale candle burns on the low table near a large photo of AFI.
KIM stands gazing out the window.
Raggedy muumuu, unkempt hair, grimy Jiffy-Lube face, runny nose.
The warplane thunders past overhead.

(KIM *looks up and waves, jumping up and down with excitement*.)

KIM. Oh! He has come back! I see his plane glide into the harbor like a – well, no actually not into the harbor is it, why'd I say 'harbor'? – plane glides into the… the – the cane fields like a – what lands in the cane fields, maybe a, a pelican…? Never mind, not the point –
At last, he has come back for us as he promised!

NARRATOR. She goes to AFI's photo, throws it down.

KIM. At last, Afi! I will leave you behind in this place and your shadow shall not fall on me anymore!

NARRATOR. AFI's ghost enters, KIM screams and falls to the floor.

AFI'S GHOST. Think again, you silly bitch!

KIM. Nooooooooooooooooooo!!

AFI'S GHOST. You better not fuck this up again because where ever you go, I go too, remember that! And I wanna go to America, dead or alive, I don't care! You'll never be free of me, I curse you for all time! You shouldn't have given me that rancid fish sandwich!

KIM. I didn't know it was rancid! Goro said it would keep at least three days!

AFI'S GHOST. I don't care! My death was still by your hand, your fishy, fishy hand! Now stop fucking around and go take a bath!

NARRATOR. She wipes her nose and runs offstage.

CLARK (*enters*) stands outside the hut with EVELYN (*his white American wife*).

CLARK. You're the best, Evelyn.

EVELYN. Yes. Yes, Clark. I know.

CLARK. How many other wives would stand by their husbands after learning of his dark island deeds?

EVELYN. Not any. But let's say no more about it, darling. We will do what we must.

We will take the child and never return to this place.

CLARK. Yes, but I need you to know that I know that you are my only –

NARRATOR. (*He breaks off as*) KIM runs in, hair wet from her bath.

KIM. My love, I knew you would not forget me!
(*She stops short when she sees* EVELYN.)
Who the fuck are you?

EVELYN (*to* CLARK). Well.
She's every bit as pretty as you said. A bit *earthy*, though.

CLARK. Kim, manolo blahnik. [Kim, it's been a long time. You look well.]
Hula puka aikau, Evelyn. [This is my wife, Evelyn.]

KIM. Your *wife*? No, no. *I'm* your wife. Remember?

(CLARK *makes a 'sorry no' face,* EVELYN *holds up her ring hand.*)

NARRATOR. KIM starts to fall to her knees, then runs into the hut instead.
She brings out the withered hibiscus crown, now a little worse for wear.

KIM. Ring any bells? No?
Surely you remember the matrimonial mango? Who could forget matrimonial mango??

CLARK. No really, I have no idea what you're – oh wait. Oh no. Oh wow.
Are you telling me that was… hoku hula? [A wedding?]

KIM. Yes, a wedding.

CLARK. Oops.

EVELYN. Clark, you know I don't speak her language. What is she saying?

CLARK. That she's my… my… wife…?

EVELYN. What?!!

CLARK. No!!

EVELYN. Then what did you just say??

CLARK. 'She's my wife…?'

EVELYN. You said 'wife'?

CLARK. No she said, 'wife' – ?

EVELYN. *How could you do this to –*

Thing is, I can't really tell what you're saying, the upward inflection is confusing me. So you're saying… she's your wife? Your – (*downward inflection*) *wife*.

CLARK. No no no no! Of course not! *You* are my only wife, Evelyn –

(KIM *gives an anguished little cry and falls to her knees again.*)

– what happened with Kim was just – you don't know how I suffered here, the darkness of the – war was in the air, the sky was – just full of – full of war and the whole island was on fire, I was on fire –

KIM. Me too – fire!

CLARK. But when I got back home, you saved me from the fire!

EVELYN (*touched by his declaration*). Oh, Clark!

KIM (*despairing*). Oh, Clark!

CLARK. Oh Evelyn!

NARRATOR. CLARK and EVELYN embrace, make out,
et cetera.

(KIM *watches them from the ground, moaning, glancing
over to see if they're done, moaning a little more*.)

Finally, KIM's resigned, walks tragically into the hut, and
returns with the prop child.

(CLARK *and* EVELYN *stare at the child.*
KIM *prostrates herself before them, her cries are still mostly
heartfelt but sometimes tapers off a tiny little bit into a tone
of 'yeah, whatever, I see how this is gonna go.'*)

KIM. Please, I beg of you! Take my son with you to America…
please!

(*Pause*.)

He must have the life I am unable to give him! Take him
away from the dirt and the, the – you know, the grime and
the greasy fish oils of this place! I'm begging you! Please, oh
please. Oh please. Oh ple–

EVELYN. Okay.

KIM. – what?

EVELYN. We'll take him.

NARRATOR. She holds out her arms, the child runs to her and
she scoops him up.

EVELYN. See you back at the plane, darling.
Don't dawdle.

(*She exits.*
KIM *weeps on the ground,* CLARK *pats her head
awkwardly*.)

CLARK. Lomi-lomi. [I'm sorry.]
Lomi, lomi, lomi-lomi. [I'm so, so sorry.]

KIM. You promise to give him everything!

CLARK. Kelikimaka! [Yes!]

KIM. Then go! Leave me!

(*He reaches for her, she turns away, he pats her and exits.*
KIM's weeping subsides, quicker than in the previous
scene.)

NARRATOR. KIM drags herself to her feet, wipes her runny
nose on her sleeve like the peasant she is, and goes into the hut.
The candle by AFI's photo has burned low, flickering.
KIM pulls AFI's abalone knife from under the futon.
She presses the point against her chest, she tests the edge of
the blade with her finger.
(*She sighs.*)
She hums a little bit of a Polynesian lullaby (*then says*):

KIM. Be the sun of my son for you are no longer mine.
The moon sinks behind the mountain.

NARRATOR. She raises the knife.
(*A beat in which we see her thinking 'Is this really the thing*
I do here…?' – then she shakes it off.)
Sudden slice across her throat,
SHNICK,
slump,
hair spreading poetically,
hand open like a fallen water lily petal.
The candle sputters and goes out.

Blackout.

1953

The final year of the Korean War, the setting for M*A*S*H, *and also in the 1950s–1960s there were a bunch of books/movies/ musicals like* The World of Suzie Wong, The King and I, *etc.*

NARRATOR. So here we are again at the busted-ass specifically vaguely Asian hut.

There's some brown hills that could be southern California or could be South Korea – both look the same, as we learned from the TV show *M*A*S*H*.
Some kinda plinky-plunky vaguely 1950s Asian music.
KIM runs on in some Asian-like streetwalker get-up, which still manages to give the impression that she works in an auto-repair shop.

(She's carrying her son/doll, and she gazes eagerly out the hut window, then stops.
She looks around the hut quickly, and down at her clothes: 'Wait just a fucking minute… wasn't I just here…?'
She shakes it off and continues with the scene, but keeps having little flashes of awareness.)

CLARK and EVELYN enter (CLARK *wears a US Army uniform*).

CLARK. Bi bim bap! [I've come back!]

KIM. You did! Four years later but okay!

CLARK. Bulgogi. (You look great, Kim.)
Chodang gol, Evelyn. [This is my wife, Evelyn.]

EVELYN. Hi.

KIM. Wow. That's… disappointing.

CLARK. We've come for my son.

KIM. Oh?

CLARK. You knew that.

KIM (*I don't like the way this seems to be going*). Maybe… or maybe not.

NARRATOR. KIM edges toward the back door, EVELYN
    boxes her out like a true center in the NBA.

EVELYN. You begged us to take him.

KIM. Did I?

CLARK. You did. Just now.
    Pakjiehae – [Remember?]

KIM. That's a name, not a verb.

CLARK. Don't you want our son to have the best life possible?

KIM. Changed my mind. He can have a below-average life here
    with me.

EVELYN. So pretty, but pretty selfish.

CLARK. Kim, be reasonable – at least I came back –

KIM. But he's my son!

CLARK. Mine too! Give me the boy!

KIM. I don't wanna!

NARRATOR. KIM turns and runs
    CLARK runs after her, wrestles her to the ground, takes the
    child and throws it to EVELYN who is back for the pass like
    an NFL wide receiver.

    (EVELYN *catches the kid and keeps running, calling back
    over her shoulder.*)

EVELYN. See ya back at the jeep, Clark!

NARRATOR. KIM weeps on the ground, CLARK pats her
    head awkwardly.

CLARK. Well.
    Kimchi. [I'm sorry.]
    Kimchi chigae. [I'm so, so sorry.]
    Uh… [Uh…]

KIM. You got what you came for, now go! Get out!

NARRATOR. He reaches for her, she slaps his hand, he exits.
    He comes back in, puts his service revolver on the ground
    beside her.

CLARK. Just in case of burglars or… raccoons.

NARRATOR. He exits.
    KIM stops crying abruptly.
    She doesn't even wipe her nose, just lets it run like the peasant she is.
    There's no dim, romantic candles flickering – it's broad daylight, harsh and unrelenting.
    She looks at the gun.

KIM. I will never see my son again.

NARRATOR. She squints up at the sun.
    She sits up, puts the gun to her temple, pulls the trigger –
    POW –
    She slumps.

    Blackout.

1975 – Part One

(*Bet you can guess why 1975. And what musical is set in Vietnam in 1975. Bet you can.*)

NARRATOR. The aforementioned hut, including the much-described vaguely Asian foolery, this time somewhere approximating Southeast Asianness.

    KIM runs on carrying her son, wearing a different set of grimy Asian pajamas.

    (*She looks at her clothes, around at the hut, realizes where/when she is.*)

KIM. Aw, crap.

NARRATOR. (*This time, she is actively – but not desperately, not yet, she has hope she can get away – looking for an escape route.*) She finds a gun just sitting in the middle of the floor.

KIM (*not gonna get me that way*). Yeah, right – not today, motherfuckers!

NARRATOR. She throws the gun out the side window (*and starts to run out the door*).

(CLARK *and* EVELYN *appear out of nowhere blocking her path, smiling, reaching for the child.*)

CLARK. Hi Kim!

Phố Bác Hồ! [Surprise! I'm back!]

KIM. No Kim here! My name is Charlene!

EVELYN. She's so pretty, just like you said –

KIM. Wrong hut! Kim is the next hut past the rubber tree!

CLARK. Bánh mì? [Is this my son?]

EVELYN. He's so cute! What a little doll! Come to Mama!

NARRATOR. She spreads her arms, the child/doll flies into them.

KIM. Give him back!

EVELYN (*to* CLARK). Meet you at the helipad, darling!

KIM. Nooooo!

(*She tries to run after them,* CLARK *grabs her.*)

CLARK. Nong, nong… [Easy now…]

KIM. It's so fucked up that you think you're saying words.

CLARK. Hey listen – it's not like I have a choice here. This hurts me just as much as it hurts you.

KIM. Oh really?

CLARK. The tide of human events has carried us away on its unjust back! You can't understand the complexity of my position – my analyst says that I'm just as much of a victim as you are –

KIM. Uh-huh.

CLARK. – because I feel so awful about this! What can I do?!
You think I like hegemony?

KIM. Well I don't know what to think, Clark! You come here, we
fall in love, we get it on, you go away for *four years*, and then
one day you just waltz back in the door?? With a *wife* – ??

CLARK. But I came back, didn't I?! I'm trying my best –

KIM. No! No! You get no points for *trying*! Fuck your trying!

CLARK. God you're hot when you're pissed off!

KIM. I'm aware!

NARRATOR. He grabs her face and lays one on her.
She fights, but the sexual chemistry is overwhelming and she
succumbs to his magic man-lips.

KIM. Oh, Clark!

CLARK. Oh, Kim!

NARRATOR. The sex happens abruptly, then a couple beats of
afterglow.

A horn honks.

CLARK. Whoops – there's my ride!
Hey um so… you stay here, I'll be right back.

NARRATOR. (*He exits*.)
KIM (*sighs*), sits on the ground, flinches, feels around in her
waistband and discovers the gun she threw out the window.

KIM. Of course. Well… fool me once…

NARRATOR. She (*sighs, exasperated*) points the gun at her
stomach.

KIM. Fool me twice, shame on me.
Shame on me.

NARRATOR. *POW!*
Slump.
Blackout.

1975 – Part Two

NARRATOR. Yeah, here again – hut, plinky music, and so
   forth.
   But KIM is onto this shit now.
   She stands in her tattered ao dai-like dress, with her Jiffy-
   Lube cheeks, looking wildly around the stage.
   EVELYN sprints across suddenly, carrying the child/doll.

KIM. Give me back my son, you bitch!

NARRATOR. KIM starts to chase her, CLARK (*appears*)
   blocks her path.
   KIM (*stumbles back, but doesn't fall, then*) notices for the
   first time there's a gun in her hand.

KIM. Oh shit –

CLARK. Oh, Kim.

KIM. Oh man.

NARRATOR. (*They look at each other.*) KIM looks around for
   an exit, there are none.

CLARK (*half-hearted*). Um – no, stop, don't.

KIM. You know what? You're right. You talked me out of it.
   I think I'll –

CLARK. Oh for god's sake –

NARRATOR. CLARK puts his hand over hers, turns the gun
   into her abdomen.
   (*She looks up at him, he's implacable.*)

KIM (*just get it over with then*). Goddammit.

NARRATOR. She squeezes the trigger –
   POW
   Blackout.

   (*The following scenes should roll through in rapid
   succession, and each time her clothes get more and more
   soaked with blood till by the end she's dripping with it –)*

1975

NARRATOR. Lights up.
AFI hands KIM a knife, she cuts her own throat.
Blackout.

1985

NARRATOR. Lights up
EVELYN hands KIM a gun, she shoots herself.
Blackout.

1995

NARRATOR. Lights up
CLARK leads KIM onto a bridge, KIM jumps.
Blackout.

2005

NARRATOR. Lights up
Oxycontin falls from the sky.

KIM. THIS IS SUCH BULLSHIT.

NARRATOR. KIM takes the pills and ODs.
Blackout – a heavy boom, like a giant door slamming shut.

Mushed-up crashed together kaleidoscopic bits of songs and
voices pulse in the dark in an arrhythmic heartbeat pattern,
kinda mesmerizing and queasy, like being squeezed through
some kind of temporal, sonic birth canal.
A great whooshing and:

2023

NARRATOR. It's twenty-fucking-twenty-three, do we think
   this makes a difference?
   Guess we'll see.

   (*In the dark, we hear easy-listening instrumental versions of
   songs like 'Bette Davis Eyes' or 'The Girl from Ipanema' for
   example.*)

   Lights up on GORO, Assistant Manager in the seafood
   section at Whole Foods in Harlem.

   He's slicing fish into fillets like a boss – seriously, he's really
   good at it and it's kinda sexy – and talking to a very old
   woman named CIO-CIO, who sullenly stacks two-for-one
   crab legs on a tray.

GORO. And my dad was a fish guy, and his dad was a fish guy,
   and *his* dad was a fish guy – yep, pretty much all the way back.
   Fish guys. What can I say, it's just in the family. And the thing
   about it is that even though the trappings of the business have
   changed – like I'm not tryna do any commercial fishing myself
   nowadays, no thank you, that shit is dangerous, I know, I saw
   Deadliest Catch and those dudes are straight-up nutso – but
   um yeah, as I say, although the accoutrements have changed,
   what with shipping and planes and whatnot, fish flying all over
   the world – you know what hasn't changed? The fish, man.
   Fish are fish. And in my family, we know fish. I can tell you
   whether a fish is fresh, what type of water it swam in – salt or
   fresh – whether it has been frozen, how far it's traveled, what
   bait they used to catch it, how old it was when it was caught,
   what it was eating, and whether it had a bad attitude – all that,
   without even looking. One small sniff and I know it all. I'm
   not bragging. Well, I guess I am, but what's wrong with that?
   In my family there was always this thing about 'no bragging'.
   If I'd even smile about my work, my dad would just – *bap* –
   up the back of my head, cuz he thought I was bragging. But
   what I think is – if you can back it up, it's not bragging. Look
   at LeBron James. And we are the best fish guys ever in the
   history of fish guys, and it's not bragging, it's the truth. We are
   the LeBron James of fish guys. The best. Period.

NARRATOR. CIO-CIO makes a movement that *might* be a shrug, continues to stack crab legs. He holds up a prawn.

GORO. Oh man she used to love these. She liked making this killer cioppino.

CIO-CIO (*grunts*).

GORO. Well, I guess that's what I'm trying to figure out. How a guy with my instincts could get so wrapped up in someone who clearly was never interested at all. I'm not gonna lie, it sorta haunts me. Like, worse than the actual fact of the break-up is the thought that somehow, I got fooled. Someone slipped me some grouper disguised as king salmon. I keep replaying what happened, trying to find clues. Should I have known? *Could* I have known? Should I have seen past her discerning taste in shellfish? Should I have known there could never be a future with her even when she talked so enthusiastically about opening a poke bar together?

CIO-CIO (*grunts*).

GORO. We were gonna call it 'Poke-Okey-Dokey'.

CIO-CIO (*grunts*).

GORO. Thanks, I did too. Anyway – all gone now, all those dreams. So strange and confusing, like... like building a house that you never get to live in. Fish don't have this problem, you know. I mean yeah they don't live in houses but also, they don't play games with love. When it's time to mate, boom. Eggs and sperm, everybody delivers the goods, no vacillating, no questions, no subterfuge. Simple. Traditional. Like me. Ahhh, well – you know. Clams in, clams out, my grandpa used to say. Any sense of control over your life is an illusion, things go the way they go, whatever will be, will be. What you gonna do? The heart wants what it wants. And in the end, it doesn't matter a whole lot, not in the greater scheme of things, like as in, if one were to consider the situation in the context of the multiverse, then who gives a shit, amiright? Through that lens, we're all just krill crawling around the ocean floor for a day. So who cares if a girl I liked, who I thought liked me, turned around and crushed me under her heel like two-for-one escargot? No one. Nobody cares and that's okay because it doesn't matter and I'm over it.

CIO-CIO (*grunts*).

GORO. For real. I'm over it.

CIO-CIO (*grunts*).

GORO. Exactly. 'Plenty of fish in the sea.'

NARRATOR. CIO-CIO pauses almost imperceptibly, makes a very slight but kindly meant pawing movement with a crab leg.
GORO nods.

GORO. Thanks. I really appreciate that.

NARRATOR. They go back to work.
CIO-CIO finishes the box of crab legs
She looks at GORO.

GORO. Done already? Wow – great job, Cio-Cio san.

CIO-CIO (*tilts her head slightly*).

GORO. No, I think that's all good. We don't seem to be that busy, so, um…
why don't you take your lunch now?

CIO-CIO (*sighs*).

GORO. It's fine, really. I'm just gonna Windex the display cases up front, then when you get back, I'll get my break.

CIO-CIO (*looks at him*).

GORO. I hear ya, Cio-Cio san. Thanks – you too.

NARRATOR. She exits into the back room.
Instrumental version of 'Let's Get It On' by Marvin Gaye starts playing, and I mean, for Muzak, the beat is slightly dope.
GORO's head starts bobbing to the beat.
Then his hips sway a bit, his shoulders bump.
Suddenly he busts out singing –

GORO. We're all sensitive people…

(GORO *sings the first verse of 'Let's Get It On'*.)

NARRATOR. At this point, bomb-ass dance moves have been fully busted, and it turns out GORO can sing the fuck outta that shit.

(GORO *keeps singing up until the refrain*.)

And so on and so forth...
Does he get down with the whole damn song with his sexy, bad-ass self? And does he grab a mic from the stack of sourdough-bread chowder bowls?
Maybe.
Does CIO-CIO enter and sing back-up vocals and do they proceed to bust a move, Motor City style?
Could be.

(*The song ends*.)

CIO-CIO san picks up her reusable grocery bag and sweater, pats GORO, and exits.
Muzak morphs into Kenny G (which doesn't sound all that different, really) and plays us out of the Whole Foods and into:
A nice apartment on a nice block on the Upper East Side, New York City.
Maybe it has the floor plan of that ol' hut, but we don't really notice that amidst all the blandly tasteful beige-sand-taupe-beach-pebble-wheat-colored Ethan Allen/Crate & Barrel/Pottery Barn puke in the room.

(*There are three doors visible: stage-right, the front door that goes to the outer hallway and elevator; stage-left, a swinging door that leads to the kitchen; and a double-door door upstage next to the cream-colored mantel over a shiny brass fireplace insert.*
There are stairs that lead to a second floor.
There are long ivory and taupe silken drapes along one wall upstage-right, behind a lovely rustic reclaimed wood bespoke dining table and chairs.
The soporific stylings of Kenny G float through.
The dining table is set for six.)

KIM stands in the center of the room, wearing a stylish
Lululemon activewear ensemble and breathing hard like she
just finished running a five-K, eyes wild and hunted, darting
around the room in confusion.
She wonders where the music is coming from – she wonders
also what IS that music, like *IS* it music, what's happening
why does it feel like someone is pouring tepid molasses into
her ears??

KIM. This isn't real.

NARRATOR. A very real sizzling and smell as ROSIE enters
from the kitchen, carrying a tray of Asian sizzling beef and
a dish of potstickers with dipping sauce and garnished with
a mango cut to look like a lotus blossom.
Oh man. It smells *delicious*.

(*The* NARRATOR *smiles and steps into the scene,* KIM *sees
her.*)

Mmmm that smells so good! Aren't you hungry, Kim?

KIM. Wait a minute… you… you're…

NARRATOR. Can I help you with anything in the kitchen,
Mrs –

ROSIE. Oh, please – call me Rosie!

NARRATOR. Sure, Rosie!

ROSIE. And you are so kind to offer, but you are a *guest*, you
are Afi's *guest* –

KIM. *Afi's* guest?? Afi is here…?

NARRATOR. Business associate, partner really – but I'm so
happy to be here. I don't get out much.

ROSIE. Yes and we are so pleased to have you here for Afi's
special night – anyway, I've got everything under control, if
I can just – Kim? Kim! What are you doing, for goodness'
sake?!

KIM. Huh?

ROSIE. Go change your clothes, we have company!! (*Smiles at* NARRATOR.) Please help yourself to wine, Brenda – we'll be ready to sit down any moment!

NARRATOR (*who we now call* BRENDA). Brenda. Huh. All right then, that's a name. I guess.

(*She grins at* KIM *and eats a potsticker*.)

BRENDA. Ohmahgah! So yummy!!

ROSIE. Thank you!

BRENDA. Where did you get these?

ROSIE. They are a special home-made recipe from my great-grandmother, who made them for her village festival every summer in the mountains of southern —

(*A burst of giggly laughter, and* EVELYN *and* AFI *enter from upstairs*.)

Oh, here they are!

EVELYN. Oh, Afi!

AFI. No, it's true, though. I would never lie to you.

EVELYN. You better *not*. Cuz I would *find out*. And then you'd be *in trouble*.

AFI. Oooo, could I please?

EVELYN. What, you silly boy?

AFI. Be *in trouble*?

(*They share a sexy-sexy look*.)
(KIM *stares at them*.)

KIM. All right then. That's new.

ROSIE. Kim!! What are you babbling about!! Go put on some decent clothes! (*Smiles at* BRENDA.) Please do have some wine!

BRENDA. Don't mind if I do. For you?

ROSIE. Oh, hee hee – no, I'm still cooking in there, don't want to set the house on fire!

BRENDA. No, we don't want that! Do we, Kim? Ha ha!
Afi, Evelyn – wine?

AFI. None for me, thanks.

ROSIE. He gets the redness. You know. In the face. And the – (*gestures to neck and chest and stomach*) all over, really.

BRENDA. Ah.

EVELYN. I think the redness is adorable.

AFI. You would, you angelic supportive weirdo. Okay then, I'll have a glass.

(*A brief canoodling.*)

ROSIE (*exiting into the kitchen*). Aww!

KIM. Eww.

AFI. Oh shut up, brat! Not like you and Clark were any different when you got engaged.

KIM….Clark? I – what? Is he – *what*?? WHERE IS HE??

AFI. Oh ha ha ha, very funny –

EVELYN. I'd love some wine, thank you, Brenda.

AFI. – and what the hell are you *wearing*? It's an engagement dinner, for god's sake! Not your, your – mooey chai class or whatever.

KIM. Can I have some wine?

BRENDA. Do you think you should?

KIM. Oh, yes, I do, I do think I should.

BRENDA. But – you're not worried about the redness – ?

KIM. I think it's safe to say the redness is the least of my worries in this moment.

BRENDA. You know, my sister is a nurse, and there is a medical and biological basis for the redness, you should really be careful about your intake of –

KIM. Sure okay.

(BRENDA *pours*.)

Yeah I'll tell you when to stop, lady.

(BRENDA *pours more*.)
(KIM *gulps down the whole glass, gestures for a refill*.)
(AFI, EVELYN, *and* BRENDA *chatter in the background,* ROSIE *clatters pots and pans in the kitchen and sizzling and steam puff into the front room through the swinging door*.)

(THE PALE ROSÉ BUBBLE.)

(KIM *sips her wine, and a pale, rosy flush steals across the stage, enclosing her in a pale rosy bubble of light.* AFI, EVELYN *and* BRENDA *sip wine and chat continuously under the following but their voices are muted, as if heard through a fabric wall*.)

Hmmmm
MmMmMmmmmHm
Sometimes I think
My body is completely separate from me
Like a
Like a
Space suit
a Me Suit
I come home from space and take off my Me Suit
and hang it on a hook on the wall
Me Suit
Where did it come from
Why do I wear it
What if I put on another one
would she be me
or he
Hmmm
Sometimes I think

I would like to go out into space without my Me Suit
Without any suit at all
Just let me be raw pink purple red jelly boneless skinless
coagulation
pulsing through space it would feel
Free
wouldn't it?
Weightless and light
But
This is ridiculous of course
No one goes out without their Me Suit
No one does that
Or
Or
Or if they *do*
If they *do* do that
go out without their Me Suit
I think
I think maybe they go and *they never come back*
(*She feels her cheeks.*)
uh ohhhhhhhh
oh noooooooooo
It's here
The Redness

(AFI, EVELYN, *and* BRENDA *invade* KIM*'s rosy bubble,
which makes a distorted 'boingy' sound as they enter.*)

AFI. I could not disagree more – it's not a serious wine.

EVELYN. Oh, Afi – you're such a purist! That's so deathly
cute.

BRENDA. I think it's a nice quaffing wine, for summer, when
it's hot –

AFI. And that's fine, Brenda, but I would never consider
cellaring a *rosé*.

I mean, come on. Why would anyone do that?

BRENDA. Why, Afi! You're a wine snob! I never knew this
about you!

EVELYN. He does have classic highbrow tastes, you should see him schooling the sommelier at Jean Georges –

AFI. If it's a crime to have a discerning palate and a taste for the best in wine – *and* women – then I am guilty as charged!

(*Tasteful laughing, quaffing – except* KIM, *who:*)

KIM (*a honk, really*). *HAH.*

BRENDA. I donno if you're guilty, but you're definitely under indictment!

EVELYN. Oh, Afi! You're so goofy! You're so mortally adorable I just wanna urrrrrr I WANNA SCRUNCH YA.

AFI. Oh? How would that work, exactly, this *scrunching* –

EVELYN. Shall I show you?

BRENDA. You guys are too much!

KIM. You said it, Brenda – (*Sotto voce to* BRENDA.) *if indeed that is your name.*

(*They all sip their wine,* KIM *chugs hers till it's gone. She stumbles over to the side table to get more – the movement causes her bubble to stretch and separate, leaving* AFI, EVELYN, *and* BRENDA *in their own bubble.*
ROSIE *comes out of the kitchen with some food, puts it on the table.*
KIM *drunkenly moves around to the couch, her rosy bubble bumps against* ROSIE, *but* ROSIE *is impervious to rosy bubbles, and does not get enveloped.*)
(ROSIE *watches* KIM *stumble to the couch, 'tsk-tsk', then she notices, through the filter of* KIM*'s bubble the* NARRATOR*'s empty chair and mic.*
She looks at the others in their bubbles, only BRENDA *notices her noticing them*
BRENDA *watches as* ROSIE *steps out of the living room, to the mic.*)

ROSIE. I would like to say at this point, that *personally*, I think this is all – it's an overreaction. But kids these days, they will

always find fault with something. It's in their nature. Fault-
finding. There is some deeply-seated need to find fault. With
everything. It has to do with the kind of people they are,
whether they are positive or negative people. I have taught
myself to be positive, to always look for the 'plus side'.

(*The bubbles around the others murmur a little 'boing
boingg'...*)

When I was young, there was movie called *The World of
Suzie Wong*. I loved this movie. And they didn't know any
better back then, so of course it's not perfect. But what is?
I can still love it.
What does that mean?
To love an imperfect thing?
I don't know.

(*Bubbles murmur.*)

I know how it felt. Like I had jumped to my feet, but inside,
in my soul. My soul jumped to its feet. To see faces that
looked like mine, in a place where I had never seen them,
somewhere I never thought they could be – an American
movie screen. With an American movie star, William
Holden, so handsome and kind. So romantic and loyal – and
for the record, it was *not* a tragic ending. He doesn't abandon
her. He defends Suzie Wong to the other bad, prejudiced
white people. He loves her, despite their many differences,
he loves her *because* of the differences. He doesn't want just
a normal wife, this man.
To me, this was wonderful.
Because – and it was just the way it was, we accepted it – we
knew that this is America. That this is not our country. We
understood that we were being allowed to live and work and
make a life in a country that did not belong to us, you see?
And yes I was born here, but being born somewhere does not
mean that you are not also a guest – every day someone asks
me where I'm from. And we try very hard to be good guests
– and to be quite honest, when I was growing up, seeing
Asian characters in films was not at the top of the list of
things we worried about. My goodness. Between raising a

family and putting food on the table, who had time for worrying about whether there were Asian characters in a movie? If I wanted to see Asian faces, all I had to do was turn sideways and *wahh* – there would be ten of them staring back at me. My parents, my brothers, my sisters, my aunts and uncles and cousins. No shortage of Asian faces in my household, believe me.

(*Bubbles murmur.*)

But you know. When that film came out. And there was this Asian woman, a Chinese woman as the star? It took my breath away and I was startled – I hadn't known how much hunger there was inside of me for that and suddenly it rose up inside of me like a storm, like a flood and I was submerged in my hunger for her face, my eyes devoured her face on that screen. All of the Asian people in that film – how hungry I was for those faces, for those lives.
And she was mixed, yes, but this only enhanced her beauty, those wide eyes with only a slight tilt upward at the corners, and she had a lovely full figure, and she was so full of life. What Asian woman wouldn't feel well-represented by such a lovely girl? And she was still so innocent, so pure, despite being forced to turn to prostitution to support her illegitimate child. And the story wasn't only about her being a – a *compromised* woman – no, no, no. Those parts of the film only lasted a few minutes here and there, and they were always very, um, blurry so you didn't see anything naughty. No, if that's all you focus on, you miss the point, that this was really a love story, about the love of a mother for her child. It showed, um, it showed the strength and nobility of soul in Asian women. Her pluck and resourcefulness and bravery. Why is it a stereotype to show that we will do anything, give everything, even our lives, for our children? Wouldn't any mother do this? Why is it bad to show that Asian women are like any other woman in this respect? I don't think it is. It is not bad to me. And she was so good that William Holden decides to marry her in the end. Even though her illegitimate baby dies in the monsoon and she is distraught with grief, she is always strong and gentle, and

William Holden rescues her from her life in Hong Kong and they live happily ever after. So there you go, you see – they do not always die in the end. Sometimes they are rescued by William Holden.

(*Bubbles murmur.*)

And all these women, these actresses, they are all so beautiful, they speak so beautifully, they are strong and good and sometimes very talented in martial arts. Even if the portrayal is not completely… factual, in a sense? It's just a story, for goodness' sake, just a movie – and for a movie, of course they will pick out the exotic aspects of our culture, it's meant to be entertaining, so people can escape their daily lives and have an adventure. And to be acknowledged at all is not… well, it is not *nothing*. And is, in fact, something to be grateful for – a crumb from the table is still food, even if it leaves you a tiny bit hungry. It is not necessarily a bad thing to be a tiny bit hungry, it gives you something to work for. I find nothing to be ashamed of in any of that. Because some of us remember a time when we were not seen at all. We were just an invisible multitude that moved across the land and *poof*! Things magically appeared! Gunpowder! The transcontinental railroad! Hand-pulled noodles!
I save my outrage for real things, things of consequence in the world. Abused children, public education, the climate crisis. How Asian people are portrayed in American culture – is it really of such concern? Does it really affect anything of consequence?

Does it?

(*Bubbles murmur.*)

Case in point: my daughter. She's…
Sometimes I wonder if she has too much freedom. And not enough struggle. So she doesn't know how to be properly grateful for either one.
She's doing some kind of internet movie with friends from the Art Institute, something about being trapped inside a mirror – or was it a window? – I can't remember, something about a

mirror that reflects a person that is not you, but then the mirror person comes alive and takes over the… something? And the real you is trapped somewhere?

The art they make, these liberal political activist types – it's all so *earnest*, so wracked with their own guilt, so angry, so intent on *putting someone in their place*. I don't know. It sounds like complete nonsense but you know – the kids these days must have their creative expression. It's unpaid, of course. Sixteen weeks of full-time work for no pay, on a depressing, angry student film. What about something nice once in a while? Why not something *happy*, like, like – *Music Man*? *Music Man* is so nice. Everyone likes *Music Man*.

(Bubbles murmur.)

Our son, on the other hand. Afi. He's doing very well, very well, indeed. He and his business partner Brenda have just gone public with their company, 'Fish in a Barrel' – can you imagine? Millions of dollars because people will pay $19.95 plus tax to eat fish and rice in a bowl for lunch. My goodness. They're opening stores all over the country. It's quite a sensation. But you know – with him, the hard work pays off. He went to Harvard Business School.

(Bubbles start rising, getting bigger.
Do we worry about popping? Maybe.)

I don't know why Kim struggles the way she does. She's her own worst enemy, you know, and I'm her mother and I love her and I don't like being the one to have to say this but if there's a choice between straight line and crooked, guess which path she always, *always* goes down. Drawn to trouble. Like a magnet. And all self-inflicted wounds as far as I can tell – her employment difficulties, dim prospects, digestive issues. Complain, complain. All day every day, just around and around in a circle. Milk gives her a stomach ache, nobody at work likes her, someone at the Whole Foods asked her where is the Chinese food aisle. I think it may have something to do with low self-esteem but I don't understand where she would have gotten that – certainly not from me. She just can't ever accept things as they are, that some things just *are the way they are*, she wants always for things to *be as they should*. Which – I have tried, over and over, to explain to her that we don't get to decide, we don't create these circumstances, they simply *are* as they *are*, and there is no use in being so rigid, so brittle. Brittle things break. You must learn to lean with the wind, not push against it in that way. You cannot win against the win. No win. No win wind. No winning with the wind, the wind wins when it wins. Bend, don't break. Stumble, don't fall. Be all you can be. If you fall behind, run faster. Fall down nine times, get up twenty, thirty, a hundred, a thousand – it doesn't matter how many times. What matters is you get up. *You get up.* YOU GET UP.

(*BZZZZT! the apartment front-door buzzer, really loud, POPS all remaining bubbles.*
ROSIE *snaps out of her reverie and goes back into the kitchen –* BRENDA *watches her.*)

(CLARK *enters, brings his own sort of golden glow into the room and he is devastatingly handsome. I mean, what the fuck? The updating of men's clothing has done only amazing things for him, he looks amazing.*)

(*His eyes meet* KIM*'s, he smiles and I mean – holy crap! He needs to stop, or everyone is going to burst into flames from his hotness.*
He crosses to KIM*, his golden glow spills over her and he lays one on her – the kiss deepens a little further than was expected, due to the aforementioned hotness, to which* KIM *is highly susceptible.*)

CLARK. The bodega didn't have any cocktail napkins, so I went to the Fairway and they had only dinner napkins, but my parents didn't raise a quitter and I said 'Oh it's ON, now!' and then what did I do?

EVELYN. I don't know! What did you do!

AFI. What!

CLARK. I Uber-ed to the fucking Paper Source on 75th and 3rd and had some finest quality organic cotton paper napkins embossed with a golden 'A' and 'E' and – BOOM! Happy engagement, kids!

AFI. That's so incredibly generous of you, man!

EVELYN. Eeeeee! Clark! You're so amazing, these look amazing, ohhhh – (*she chokes back tears, to* BRENDA) Don't these look *amazing*??

BRENDA. Awwwww! The little golden A and E! For Afi –

BRENDA/EVELYN. – and Evelyn!! Awwwww!!

(ROSIE *bursts back in with yet another platter of food*.)

ROSIE. Perfect timing!

(*Everyone cheers, golden light glints off the package of napkins as* CLARK *joins the party; he opens the package and expertly fans the napkins, placing them artfully on a side table with the beverages*.)
(KIM *watches as everyone floats over to the dinner table, bits of conversation float around as they eat and talk and laugh in golden slow motion.*
KIM'*s rosy glow wears off somewhere in the middle of dinner,*

right about here →)

CLARK. And then I said, 'Hey man, you better tie your shoe!'

(*They all laugh hysterically*.)

ROSIE. Oh, Clark! You're so funny!

AFI. Hilarious, man!

EVELYN. I love the way you tell stories!

(*Laughing, laughing.*
CLARK *glances over at* KIM, *who is standing in the same spot*.)

CLARK. Sweetheart, come sit down.

(KIM *doesn't move*.)

AFI. 'Hey man – '

CLARK/AFI. 'You better tie your shoe!'
   AH HAH AHAHAHAHAHHAHAHAHHHH!!

(CLARK *looks at* KIM.)

   Kim. Honey? Earth to Kim, come in, Kim –

ROSIE. Kim!! Your husband is talking to you!

KIM. Yeah… I don't think so…

AFI. Oh my god.

EVELYN. Is she all right?

BRENDA. She's maybe been through a lot… lately…?

EVELYN. Oh. Has she tried therapy? Because I know a terrific
   therapist, down in the East Village –

CLARK. Anyway – I'd like to make a toast.

   (*They all look at him.*)

   When I first met Afi, he was being stuffed into a recycling
   bin behind the dining hall by the varsity lacrosse team, and
   I thought how strange it was that a grown man could fit into
   a recycling bin.

   (*Laughter around the table.*)

   And I was also glad that I played rugby because those
   lacrosse guys ended up getting suspended later that year for
   setting fire to the arts and humanities library.

   (*Laughter.*)

   But I digress. And all kidding aside, I made a new friend that
   day, and though I didn't know it, also the person who would
   introduce me to the love of my life.

   (*Murmuring, 'awww', etc.*)

   Afi and Evelyn. If you have even half the happiness I've
   found with Kim, you will be the luckiest couple on earth.

ROSIE. Hear, hear!

BRENDA. That was so nice! So nicely put!

ROSIE. You have such a gift with words, Clark!

(*They all drink the toast.*)

KIM. *Hah!*

BRENDA. Pardon me?

KIM. Thass was a hoot! Thass what thass was!

(*Buzzkill.* ROSIE *glares at her.*)

A… hoooo… t…

(*Pause.*)

Yeahhp… thiss the nice part, I guess. Where everyone is… happy… wedding mochi…

AFI. Can you please get a grip?

KIM. Oh, Afi. Afi, Afiiiiii. I sorry that sandwich was rancid. I dint mean that to you.

AFI. Oh my god – what are you talking about?

KIM. I know, I know – this your happy time, iss the happy time. Shhh. I know what comes next, but I won't say. So you can enjoy your happy time. Especially all the – (*makes vulgar fucking gesture*) yeahhhhhh, baby. Go 'head. Get it, Afi.

ROSIE. Kim…

KIM. Yep, thass my name, so they say, but let's look into that a lil bit, shall we? Why is so many Asians call 'Kim' in this place? Huh? Why so Asian name here? Iss not even a girl's name, iss a LAST NAME, a SURNAME, why's name girl baby 'Kim'?? Shhh, so dumb. Iss *Korean*, iss KOREAN LAST NAME, what you gonna do, name girl KIM KIM?? Hahhhhh iss fuckin *joke*.
Thass for start.

AFI. Mom – make her stop –

KIM. And oh yeah I juss remember –

ROSIE. KIM!! STOP IT!!

KIM. I AM NOT LOTUS FLOWER!! OR EXOTIC
INNOCENCE MODEL MINORITY DOCILE!! OR LUCY
LIU!! Or A&P class girl Grace Chung. Or barista Louisa
Changchien.

CLARK. Just let her go, maybe she'll get it out of her system.

KIM. I also donno where is the best Chinese food nearby. And
I'm not fluent in Japanese. I don't wanna die so my son can
have a better life. I just I just I just –

EVELYN (*like the Dog Whisperer*). Oh, Kim. Shhh. Shhh now.

KIM. I'm just me –

EVELYN. I know you're in pain.

KIM. – why does it always happen… why do I always… why
does it always end the same way…?

EVELYN. Hey, I get it, I know.

KIM. Oh? Do you?

AFI. Evelyn, you don't have to engage with her when she's like
this. It's very sweet of you to try but –

EVELYN. I know, because as a *woman*, as a fellow sufferer of
injustice, I have been where you are, Kim.

BRENDA (*maybe not, lady*). Mmm – has she…?

ROSIE (*under her breath*). Well maybe she has, she's done
everything else.

(BRENDA *and* ROSIE *cackle and slyly give each other dap*.)

EVELYN. The hardest thing in the world is to resist striking
back when you feel like things are so unfair, like the world
isn't being very fair, you feel like, 'Hey, I'm doing all the
right things, why aren't you being fair?' I know.

KIM. Hey lady *you donno know me*.

EVELYN. I know you have hurt. We all do. We've all been through so much, haven't we? As a woman, as a feminist, I know these battles – I have fought them my whole life! Not being chosen as Senior Class President though I was much more qualified than the *boy* they elected! Being second in my class at Harvard! Driving a hand-me-down BMW that didn't even have a sunroof! Keys to an executive washroom which is *two doors* away from my office instead of part of the suite like the other VPs! Being passed over again and again for CEO! Beauty is wound, my friend – my goodness, the judgement we endure just because we know how to apply a little lipstick! So look – I know the corrosive nature of the struggle for acceptance and validation and autonomy, what that can do to your faith in humanity, and I know how difficult it is to keep the faith when the world wants to put its limits on you, to define you in their small box marked 'Woman' or 'Wife' or 'Chorus Dancer' –

KIM. uh-huh

EVELYN. But I believe in you, Kim. I believe that you can be strong enough to put yourself aside, and hold space to celebrate with Afi and me. To know that whatever you have experienced in the past, in this room, you are loved and accepted for who you are, and your truth is honored. I know what you've been through. I've been there, believe me – I have been there.

> (*Pause.*
> KIM *looks at* EVELYN *with intensity, it's not clear if she's thinking about hugging her or strangling her.*)

CLARK. Sweetheart, please – can we just all go sit together and celebrate this wonderful union?

> (*Silence.* CLARK *and* EVELYN *exchange a meaningful glance,* EVELYN *crosses back to* AFI, *squeezes* CLARK*'s arm as she passes.*)

KIM. *I saw that.*

BRENDA. Oh boy.

CLARK. Kim, please calm down.

KIM. You think I don't know what's going on here?

CLARK. Come sit, I promise you, there's nothing –

EVELYN. Clark. Tell her the truth.

CLARK. What??

EVELYN. I told Afi. And he's fine with it.

AFI. Yes. I'm fine with it. I'm cool like that.

EVELYN. It was before Afi and were together, of course.

AFI. But I'm cool with it. It happens, you know.

CLARK. Wow.

KIM. Uh-huh. And…?

CLARK. Kim, this is… well it was a long time ago…

EVELYN. Not that long. Not really.

KIM.…that you and Evelyn were fucking…

ROSIE. Don't say 'fucking' it's so vulgar! Say 'had an affair' –

CLARK. Yes so, we had an affair –

KIM. After we were married.

CLARK. Maybe…?

KIM. Yeah.

CLARK. But it ended! That's the most important part of the story, it ended! And we, Evelyn and I, agreed it was a terrible mistake!

KIM. Did you? That's too bad.

CLARK. I know it's a lot to take in, and I didn't want you to ever have to know, but… in the interest of transparency – I'm so sorry, Kim –

KIM. Okay.

CLARK. What?

EVELYN. What?

KIM. I know you and Evelyn used to fuck, and I don't care. Can we move on?

CLARK. Oh. Uh. Okay.

AFI. Huh. Interesting. I would have expected a bigger reaction.

KIM. Well, Afi. I guess I'm cool like that.

AFI. Yeahh… okay…

EVELYN. Well it's really a relief to have it all out in the open –

ROSIE. Of course, and it doesn't mean anything! Now we can have all the incomes in one big family, and we'll all gather in the Hamptons for the holidays every year with the –

KIM. NOPE!!!!!!!

(KIM *throws her glass at the wall.*
Stunned silence, everyone stares at her.)

I know what you're doing, you assholes. Trying to make me think that I'm – drive me to – you know – SCHNICK!!

ROSIE. Language, Kim!

AFI. Mom, don't start on her. It won't help.

ROSIE. Well.

KIM. Stop talking about me like I'm not here!!

AFI. Hey! How about you calm down!!

(CLARK *crosses to* KIM, *who backs away warily.*)

KIM. I think I'm gonna go now.

CLARK. Kim, come on – your mother made this wonderful food for everyone. Don't you want to sit and eat?

KIM. Nope!!

CLARK. Kim –

KIM. I'm not falling into your traps!! Not again!! HOW STUPID DO YOU THINK I AM??!!

CLARK (*moves closer to her, hands out to her*). Shh, shh – no one thinks you're stupid –

KIM. Hey! You better *fall back*, buddy –

CLARK. Come on now. It's me. Clark. I would never –

KIM. HAH!!

ROSIE. Kim, stop being ridiculous and come eat your dinner.

KIM. How could *you* do this, this – all of this!? You're my *mother*!

ROSIE. Oh, here we go again –

KIM. How could you let me be *sold to a* –

ROSIE. – it's all my fault, everything is my fault, all your failures, all your pain and worry and problems, all me, not you, it's always my fault –

KIM. YOU WERE SUPPOSED TO PROTECT ME!!

ROSIE. Enough of this silliness. Kim, calm down immediately and stop embarrassing the family in front of company!!

CLARK. Kim, darling –

(CLARK *makes a move to grab her, she dodges him and runs to the front door, stage-right (1), scrabbles at the handle, gets it open and runs out.*
Everyone looks at each other: EVELYN *looks concerned in the way of sisterhood,* BRENDA *looks concerned, narratively speaking,* ROSIE *eats sizzling beef,* AFI *shrugs.*)

(KIM *runs back on, coming in from upstairs.*
She looks around in dismay.)

KIM. Crap!

CLARK. Kim! Wait!

(KIM *sprints out the front door (1) again, again runs on from upstairs.*
She looks around, out of breath.)

KIM. Are you fucking *kidding me*???

(*She runs out the kitchen swinging doors, stage-left (2), comes back on through the front door.*)

GAAAAHHHHHH!!!!

(*She runs up the stairs but enters through the kitchen doors.*)

(*Out of breath.*) God. Dammit.

(*She runs to the double-doors upstage (3), wrenches them open and out tumbles an avalanche of dark bamboo screens, low table, palm fronds – detritus from the earlier scenes in the love hut, including an array of the weapons used in the suicides.*)

The fuck is this shit??! Some kinda twisted *recycling program*?!!

CLARK. Now, Kim – let's stay calm –

KIM. You know, it's funny how often in my life people have said that to me. And what I think is, actually, I *am* calm. I'm already a pretty calm person, a quiet person. I keep my TV at a low volume, I don't use my cellphone in public, I try to approach people in the least threatening way possible even if it's to ask them to take their foot off my windpipe – and maybe being *quiet* is not the same as being *calm*, but. I think that's what you actually mean, right? You want me to be quiet. To SHUT UP. To not raise questions or a fuss or my own son. To die beautifully, tragically, nobly, sacrificially, and silently. I might as well not be here at all, you could use my Me Suit.

ROSIE. Your what?

KIM. Not important. Anyway. Oh lookee what we have here.

(KIM *picks up a gun from the junk on the floor. The others gasp.*)

I know how it ends and *I don't wanna do this anymore*. Now which one of you assholes is gonna to tell me how to get out of this shitshow?

(BRENDA's *eyes involuntarily glance at the drapes along the upstage-left wall*.)

AH-HAH!!!

CLARK. Please, Kim. Just – sit with me and talk. We can –

(*He blocks her way, lunges, a struggle for the gun which* CLARK *wins, he throws it away.*
KIM s*prints away, he chases her around the room,* AFI *and* ROSIE *and* EVELYN *join in, trying to corral* KIM *like she's a runaway horse.*
BRENDA *sips wine and watches*.)

KIM. Y'ALL BETTER GET OUTTA MY WAY IF YOU DON'T WANNA END UP ON THE FLOOR – !!

EVELYN. Stop, Kim – you don't know what you're doing –

AFI. Clark's a good guy, Kim!! He's stood by you all this time!! Why are you putting him through this?!!

ROSIE. You spoiled brat!! I knew we should've drowned you in the well!!

I mean the hospital!! Left you in the hospital!!

KIM. AAAAAAAAAAAAA!!!!

(KIM *lowers her shoulder NFL-tackle-style and lays them out, one by one, until only* CLARK *is left between her and the drapes.*
She fakes left and goes right, but he's got some defense and he boxes out.
And yeah, I've again mixed NFL and NBA terminology in the same paragraph of stage directions. So what. That's the least of your worries, at this point.)

(*A standoff.*)

Move.

CLARK. No.

KIM. *Move. Your ASS. OUT OF MY WAY.*

CLARK. NO. I'm not giving up on us.

(KIM *laughs mirthlessly*.)

KIM. Is that what you think this is about? You giving up or not giving up?

CLARK. Well… uh…

KIM. Get out of my way, Clark.

CLARK. No, Kim! I can't let you go, I love you too much! I will always love you in spite our differences, in spite of the difficulty of trying to understand you and – *why*?? Why are you like this?

KIM. GOOGLE IT, MOTHERFUCKER!!

(KIM *makes a move to get past, he blocks her*.)

CLARK. Shh I need you to stop yelling and calm down –

KIM. TOLD Y'ALL TO STOP TELLING ME TO CALM DOWN OR – !!

AFI. Or what? What are you gonna do??

KIM. *You have no idea what I can do to you, Afi.*

AFI. Oh come on –

KIM. *Would you like a fish sandwich??*

(AFI *blanches*.)

BACK THE FUCK UP.

CLARK. I feel like you're determined to make me the bad guy here, and I honestly don't know what I did to deserve that. If you could just – explain to me why you feel this way –

KIM. IT'S NOT ABOUT MY FEELINGS, ASSHOLE!! STOP MAKING IT SEEM LIKE I AM THE PROBLEM HERE AND YOU'RE SO REASONABLE!!

BRENDA. Kim –

KIM. YOU.

BRENDA. Me?

KIM. Yes, you, don't play like you don't know.

(BRENDA *gazes at her placidly, starts putting food in her pockets.*)

BRENDA. Welp. Been nice having a break, but I suppose it's about time we get back. Don't worry. All of this is gonna play through, the way it always does, and you won't remember.

KIM. I remember you. *I know you know what I know.* You do! You know!

BRENDA. Do I?

KIM. You saw it! In the hut! The *huts*!! All those times, every single time! I was alone and you saw! And you wouldn't help me…? Why wouldn't you do something, you knew, you saw it – why why??? Aaaaaaaaaa…

(*She has flashbacks of* CLARK *leaving her, taking her child, the suicides – this pain starts to have a tinge of reality, poignancy.*)

It happened, it happened, it happened to me, it's in me – it's not wiped away, it stays somewhere, you know – it stays inside me, every time. Every time. With the knife, with the gun, down the well, off the bridge, the poison, the fire, the water, the hands around my neck, the sword through my belly, the rape, the beating, the hanging, the pillow over my face – I remember them all. I remember them all. The way I was torn, and crushed, and dragged, and burned, and cut. I feel it in my body, all those deaths. Over and over and over. But that wasn't the worst.
Not the worst.
The worst…
My son… alive in my body, then warm in my arms, his little hands, his tiny fingers clasped around my thumb like a starfish all night, all the nights I didn't sleep, waiting for his father to come back, dreaming of the world outside that hut. And when they came, when they took him from me, when

they tore him from my body, his hands his feet his cheeks,
everywhere his little body touched mine he took my skin on
his skin when they pulled him away and I was left peeled
and raw, missing skin a red patchwork on my body angry
bleeding burns in the shape of him.
That.
Over and over.
Do you have any idea what that feels like?
Can you even imagine?

(*Pause.*)

Now how do I get out of here??

BRENDA. Ah. See, this is where I think you are a little
confused and you don't understand that –

KIM. WAY OUT!!

BRENDA. – YOU'RE ALREADY OUT! THIS IS OUT!!

KIM. It can't be… no… this can't be all there is, I…

(*Beat.*
KIM *sprints over and pulls the drapes aside, revealing
a sliding glass door – harsh searing white light floods the
stage, bleaching everything and obscuring what lies beyond
the door.*)
(KIM *and* BRENDA *exchange a long look,* KIM *slides the
door open.*
Wind blows in.
KIM *tries to see what's beyond the door, but she can't see
anything.*)

What about this?

(BRENDA *shrugs.*)

BRENDA. I honestly don't know.

(*Do we believe her?
I don't know.*)

We could stop here. We could stay here. It's not so bad, is it?

(KIM *stands on the threshold, the wind blows harder.*
She's scared.
She looks at BRENDA, *then takes one step across the*
threshold.
Lights flare white-hot and burn everyone's eye sockets and
KIM *disappears from view.*)

(*Blackout.*)

(*We could stop here.*)
(*We could stay here.*)
(*Or…*)
(*In the black, a sound comes up, waves of a sound that*
slowly resolves into a voice, a very distorted and slowed-
down voice…

Lights and sound bump up –)

GORO. Hey! Hey, Kim! Come on, girl, wake up!

(KIM *opens her eyes and she's in the seafood section at*
Whole Foods in Harlem.)
(*She's lying on the floor,* GORO *leaning over her,*
concerned.)

Oh my god!

(KIM *sits up slowly.*)

Are you okay? How do you feel? Okay? Not okay? Do you
want me to call someone for you? Call 911?

KIM. Goro…?

GORO. Yeah, hi, hi – I just – are you okay?

KIM. Yeah…?

GORO. Oh my god, girl – shit was *crazy* – you came in and like
you were yelling and running and – like someone was
chasing you, right? Like straight-up yelling and carrying on
and throwing seafood condiments and sourdough chowder
bowls at people, and I was like 'Oh shit, it's Kim' and you
were like '*Lemme outta here, you assholes!! You don't know*
who I am!!' and I was like 'But I *do* know who you are!!

Come down off the sushi display case please!!' and then
right when the store manager was about to call the cops you
just – PADONK! You just like passed the fuck out right on
top of the crab legs display and fell to the floor and then we
had to get a – never mind, not important – and then you were
just laying there for like, the last twenty minutes and then,
and then – and then you woke up.

KIM. Where…?

GORO. The seafood section at the Whole Foods in Harlem.
New York.

KIM. Harlem.

GORO. New York.

(KIM *looks around*.)
(GORO *watches her closely*.)

KIM. I… don't think I've been in this one before.

The layout is… different.

GORO. Yeah, you go to the one in Columbus Circle, right?
Yeah. I get it – they got an escalator.
Hey, are you…? Are you sure you're okay? What year is it?
Who is the President of the – no that's too disappointing to
think about –
Okay – where do you live?

(KIM *looks around*.)

Or maybe, how many fingers am I holding up?

KIM. Goro.

GORO. Nope, it's two. Oh god, I hope there's no permanent
damage –

KIM. Goro.

GORO. – okay how about – What's my name? Do you know me?

KIM. …Goro.

GORO. That's right! That's good, so your memory is pretty,
um, I guess, intact or whatnot if you can remember me –

KIM. I've known you longer than I've known almost anybody.

GORO. Yeah. You have.

(*Pause*.)

Well… do you wanna… come in the back, chill in the break room for a minute?

KIM. Am I allowed in the back room?

GORO. Hey, I am the seafood section assistant manager. I do what I want.

(GORO *helps her up*.)

You want some water, something to eat? Some like, soup or whatnot?

KIM. I think I just need to… sit for a minute?

GORO. There's a couch back there, and you can chill as long as you need to, and then whenever you want, you can leave.

KIM. That's – that's perfect.

GORO. Lemme know if you want me to call you an Uber, or whatever.

(*Pause*.)

Funny. I was just talking about you today.

KIM. Oh yeah?

GORO. Yeah.
Now here you are.

KIM. Here I am now.

(*They start moving toward the back room*.)

GORO. Hold up. Ima get you a smoothie.

KIM. Uh…

GORO. We got these new fruit smoothies – I'll get you one but you don't hafta drink it, if you don't wanna, but you'll probably wanna because that shit is delicious and it's probably good for your, your blood sugar and whatnot.

KIM. Okay. Thanks. I don't have my wallet with me but –

GORO. Don't worry about it – I got you. Be right back.

(GORO *exits*.
KIM *waits*.)

(CIO-CIO *san enters, sees the destroyed crab leg display.*
She sighs deeply.
She and KIM *see each other.*
A moment.
KIM *nods at her.*
CIO-CIO *san nods back*.)

KIM. CIO-CIO san smiles suddenly, a huge, bright, joyful smile that touches and warms everything in the vicinity.

She lifts a hand and makes some kind of vague circle motion in the air that encompasses the busted crab legs display, the seafood section, KIM, GORO, the whole store, the whole world, and which means:

'Every day we must begin anew.
This is what it is to be alive.'

(*She and* KIM *smile at each other.*)
(*Muzak plays, maybe 'O-O-H Child' by The Five Stairsteps.*)

(*Blackout.*)

(*End of mutherfucking play.*)

A Nick Hern Book

untitled fuck miss saigon play first published in Great Britain in 2023 as a paperback original by Nick Hern Books Limited, The Glasshouse, 49a Goldhawk Road, London W12 8QP, in association with the Royal Exchange Theatre, Factory International for Manchester International Festival, Young Vic Theatre and Headlong

Front cover: Image Design by Émilie Chen. Photography by Trần Quốc Bảo (Pexels)

Designed and typeset by Nick Hern Books, London
Printed in Great Britain by Mimeo Ltd, Huntingdon, Cambridgeshire PE29 6XX

A CIP catalogue record for this book is available from the British Library

ISBN 978 1 83904 241 6

www.nickhernbooks.co.uk/environmental-policy

www.nickhernbooks.co.uk

 facebook.com/nickhernbooks

 twitter.com/nickhernbooks